The Sunset At McCook

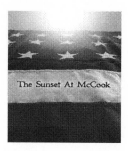

Rodney L. Kelley

2020

D1157336

I

Rodney L. Kelley
Harrisburg, Pennsylvania
rodkelley@comcast.net

Note: This is a work of nonfiction. No names have been changed, no characters invented, no events fabricated.

The Sunset At McCook/Rodney L. Kelley -- 1st ed.

ISBN 978-0-578-73375-3

"I shall never forget the sunset at McCook."

Franklin Delano Roosevelt
Poughkeepsie, New York
November 7, 1932

August 2020

President Carter,
        thank you for your service to
our country!

        All the best!
        Rudy Kinny

Contents

The Sunset At McCook

The Sunset At McCook

The Sunset At McCook

I – Introduction

"I know where I was 50 years ago, I was on the prairie fairgrounds in McCook, Nebraska, looking at the most brilliant sunset I had ever seen. I was listening to a couple of speakers whose hushed tones caught the awesome feeling of the sky. One of them was FDR (who was running for President), and the other was saintly Senator George Norris. What was the secret of his power? I don't know. Yes, I remember the date. It was September 28, 1932, half a century ago. Overhead, the sky throbbed and pulsed."[1]

This book explores this event pondered half a century later by Richard Strout, a Pulitzer Prize-winning reporter, who covered the presidential campaign of that year. In the pages that follow, we look closely at that speech and the vision of civic service espoused by Franklin Delano Roosevelt (FDR) that evening in the Senator's home town.

Our story begins at approximately 7:15 p.m. on Wednesday, September 28, 1932, almost nine decades ago with a middle-aged presidential candidate sitting on the backseat of an open chauffeured auto borrowed from an Omaha attorney's family.[2] In the middle of a

---

[1] TRB. *Adventure in Socialism*, Baltimore, Maryland: Baltimore Sun, September 27, 1982, p. 11.
[2] *Democratic Leaders Are Hard Put to Find an Open Car for Roosevelt*, Omaha, Nebraska: Omaha World-Herald, September 28, 1932, p. 8.

campaign swing through the western United States, FDR savored the sunny picture-perfect late autumn weather astride the 98th Meridian in this semiarid section of the Cornhusker state.[3]

Unexpectedly, as his vehicle was departing the facility where he had given a speech moments before, he asked the driver to halt. Forrest Burbank, a 22-year-old Harvard College graduate and Creighton University law student, whose father owned the car, followed his wishes.[4] The politician gazed spellbound to the west.

Following his decision, an amphitheater of interested faces surrounding the candidate's car focused on the splash of bright colors in the atmosphere, which quickly overshadowed the rapidly receding daylight. Approximately 20,000 people were in attendance, which was the most significant outpouring ever gathered in this part of Nebraska to that time.[5] They watched transfixed as Governor Franklin Delano Roosevelt (FDR) of New York surveyed the sky for a quarter-hour in silence, fascinated by a crescendo of color in the heavens.

---

[3] Neal Pierce. *The Great Plains States of America,* New York, New York: W. W. Norton and Company, 1973, p. 210.

[4] *Margaret Hurd Bride Of Forrest Browne Burbank*, Lincoln, Nebraska: Lincoln Star, June 9, 1934, p. 2.

[5] George Frank Fisher. *Roosevelt At McCook*, Lincoln, Nebraska: Lincoln Star, September 29, 1932, p. 13.

I – Introduction

The view, which mesmerized the crowd, formed as the sun traveled over the Pacific Ocean halfway between Asia and North America. That afternoon it drove its rays across thousands of miles from that point to the United States, allowing half of the country to enjoy the same beautiful phenomenon. These conditions set the stage for a cascading atmospheric chain of events culminating with a stunning late-day natural spectacle in Nebraska.

In practical terms, the light from the sun midway across the Pacific Ocean scattered molecules over thousands of miles as it beamed through the atmosphere.[6] When the ball of light crept below the horizon, the earth's upper atmosphere reflected the sunlight and illuminated the lower sky. The sight of this spectacle at McCook was a western twilight abounding in vivid shades of gold and red streaking through the atmosphere.

The effect on the crowd was awe-inspiring and stayed with many of them for the rest of their lives.[7]

---

[6] Stephen F. Cordi. *The Colors of Sunset and Twilight*, web page: https://www.spc.noaa.gov/publications/corfidi/sunset, accessed February 2020.

[7] Richard L. Strout. *The Enduring Legacy Of Franklin Roosevelt*, Washington, D.C.: Washington Post, October 23, 1983, web site: http://www.washingtonpost.com/archive/entertainment/books/1983/10/23/the-enduring-legacy-of-franklin-d-roosevelt/732914d-a983-4cd2-aff3-2519bc0939be/, accessed February 2020.

The Sunset At McCook

Numerous newspapers across the country described this magnificent sunset in their Thursday, September 29, edition. One reporter who viewed the spectacle portrayed the phenomenon as, "Almost religious…like being in a cathedral."[8]

This visit occurred on the 17th day of a railroad campaign trip through the far west. Mr. Roosevelt started the day in Colorado, making whistle-stops along the railroad, as he traveled to Nebraska as part of his campaign to be inaugurated as the 32nd President of the United States.[9] His schedule called for his visit to last approximately 2 ½ hours.[10]

An estimated 20,000 people, scarcely one-third of whom could find seats in the 4,500 person grandstand, waited for the dignitaries at the fairground on the edge of McCook.[11] Twilight was falling over the

---

[8] Richard L. Strout. *The Enduring Legacy Of Franklin Roosevelt*, Washington, D.C.: Washington Post, October 23, 1983, web site: http://www.washingtonpost.com/archive/entertainment/books/1983/10/23/the-enduring-legacy-of-franklin-d-roosevelt/732914d-a983-4cd2-aff3-2519bc0939be/, accessed February 2020.

[9] Richard L. Strout. *The Enduring Legacy Of Franklin Roosevelt*, Washington, D.C.: Washington Post, October 23, 1983, web site: http://www.washingtonpost.com/archive/entertainment/books/1983/10/23/the-enduring-legacy-of-franklin-d-roosevelt/732914d-a983-4cd2-aff3-2519bc0939be/, accessed February 2020.

[10] James A. Hagerty. *Roosevelt Urges End Of Party Lines*, New York, New York: New York Times, September 29, 1932, p. 10.

[11] *Norris Called Ideal Liberal By Roosevelt*, Baltimore, Maryland: Baltimore Sun, September 29, 1932, p. 1.

I - Introduction

plains as the crowd jammed into the high-roofed bandstand directly in front of the speaker's rostrum. They spilled onto the grounds and formed into a circle about it.[12]

Roosevelt stood in the dust of the track supported by his sedan. The orator faced the grandstands with a microphone to his front. Workers turned on the roof lights as the sun receded, sending a glaring light down upon the candidate and a nearby American flag as he stood in a rope-enclosed area.[13] The bulk of the crowd followed the proceedings from loudspeakers set up throughout the grounds. The speeches began at about 6:30 p.m.

The crowd dramatically swelled the population of this railroad and farmers' shopping center perched on the rolling prairie of Western Nebraska. Festooned with flags and bunting this day was a novel occurrence in its history. With its population tabulated in 1930 at 6,688, the crowd temporarily increased the populace of the five square mile community by almost threefold.[14] In proportion to people, it was the

[12] W. B. Ragsdale. *Norris Praises Governor Roosevelt As Needed Man,* Lincoln, Nebraska: Lincoln Journal Star, September 29, 1932, p. 2.
[13] W. B. Ragsdale. *Nebraska Solon Bolts Party To Back Democrats,* Owensboro, Kentucky: Owensboro Messenger, September 29, 1932, p. 2.
[14] *Norris Called Ideal Liberal By Roosevelt,* Baltimore, Maryland: Baltimore Sun, September 29, 1932, p. 1.

biggest crowd Governor Roosevelt had drawn to this point in the campaign.[15]

The attendees, drawn from rural communities in Nebraska, Kansas, and Colorado, were captivated by his charisma and the spectacle of a presidential campaign.[16] Delegations streamed out of the North Platte valley from Chadron and Valentine, from Hastings, Holdrege, and North Kansas counties.[17] Many listeners were farmers savaged since 1929 by the Great Depression and chronic droughts.

Countless attendees with political banners on their cars journeyed 50 to 100 miles on rough country roads for the approximately hour-long event. Their journey was remarkable, given that these Midwesterners could have easily stayed home and listened to the speech. Roosevelt's remarks were broadcast on the radio to the nation by the National Broadcasting Corporation (NBC).[18] These concerned citizens made the arduous trek even though this was the first day of the baseball World Series.[19] Many residents did so because

---

[15] Edward W. Gableman. *After You*, Cincinnati, Ohio: Cincinnati Inquirer, September 29, 1932, p. 9.

[16] John Boettinger. *Roosevelt and Norris Swap Trade Lasts*, Chicago, Illinois: Chicago Tribune, September 29, 1932, p. 1.

[17] W. B. Ragsdale. *Norris Praises Governor Roosevelt As Needed Man*, Lincoln, Nebraska: Lincoln Star, September 29, 1932, p. 5.

[18] Associated Press, *Senator Norris To Welcome Demo Chief To State*, Lincoln, Nebraska: Lincoln Star, September 28, 1932, p. 1.

[19] David J. Walsh. *Gotham All Set To Start Series*, Lincoln, Nebraska: Lincoln Star, September 28, 1932, p. 11.

I – Introduction

Franklin Delano Roosevelt, the Democratic party candidate, gave them
what they longed for, hope for the future.

The memories of that event lingered for generations throughout
the southwestern Nebraska region. Later that year, in November, after
winning the presidency, FDR, in a speech at Poughkeepsie, New York,
affirmed that among his treasured memories of the recent campaign was
the sunset on that day in McCook, Nebraska.[20] As late as the early
2000s, a local newspaper published an article describing the event and its
significance in McCook's history.[21]

As the unbelievable sunset pealed over the prairie, its vivid
colors aggrandized the themes of the speech. One of the most
memorable refrains came when Democrat Franklin Roosevelt lauded
McCook resident and republican/independent the United States Senator
George Norris. Governor superbly defined what constituted true
greatness in a public official.[22] The New York Times was one of several
national publications that transcribed the speech in full the next day.[23] It
stands the test of time as a model for excellence in public administration.

---

[20] Franklin Delano Roosevelt. *Poughkeepsie, New York Informal Speech*,
November 7, 1932, p. 3.
[21] Linda Hein. *Remembering A True Gentleman*, McCook, Nebraska:
McCook Gazette, February 1, 2002, p. 1.
[22] Richard L. Neuberger and Stephen B. Kahn. *Integrity, The Life Of George
W. Norris*, New York, New York: Vanguard Press, 1937, p. 300.
[23] Associated Press. *Roosevelt's Speech At McCook*, New York, New York:
New York Times, September 29, 1932, p. 10.

One notable example of its resilience occurred almost thirty years later. President-elect John Fitzgerald Kennedy evoked similar dogmas in his farewell speech to the General Court of Massachusetts on January 09, 1961. He invoked the leadership principles of FDR, stated at McCook, as he prepared to take the oath of office for the nation's highest political position.[24]

This document is a chronicle of the legacy of that speech. It highlights pertinent segments of the narrative and illustrates its lasting impact on United States Congressional policymakers.

Finally, this narrative honors the efforts of all who place integrity, unselfishness, courage, and consistency as the guiding principles of their public service.

---

[24] Lambert Lane. *Remembering JFK's Farewell Speech To Massachusetts*, Quincy, Massachusetts: Patriot Ledger, January 9, 2011.

II - The Roosevelt Special

The newly-minted Democratic party candidate for President of the United States, Governor Franklin Delano Roosevelt of New York, met with his campaign staff in early September 1932. Their goal was to design an initiative to capture enough electoral votes in ordinarily Republican states to win the contest with the incumbent, Herbert Hoover, in November.[1] These seasoned political operatives advised that the Midwest and West were favorable territories for the national ticket for the first time in sixteen years. Roosevelt and his team fathomed a journey to whip up enthusiasm in states that had not been carried by a Democratic candidate since 1916.

They designed a whistle-stop journey, which was the first of its extensive nature in many years. Roosevelt stated, "I am stubborn, and I like to travel," when asked about his plans and seemed to relish the idea of going out through the nation and making a personal appeal. The time table of the special train described a schedule that began with a departure from Albany on September 12 covering 8,900 miles and traversing twenty-one states stopping for speeches mostly throughout

---

[1] *Roosevelt Leaves On Trip To Coast*, New York, New York: New York Times, September 12, 1932, p. 1.

the western half of the country.[2] The schedule called for him to return to Albany on October 3.

As scheduled, New York Governor Franklin Delano Roosevelt (FDR) set out by railroad from Albany, New York, on the three-week late-summer journey. The self-titled "look, listen and learn" tour included planned policy speeches on the farm crisis, railroads, electric power, industrial policy, and the tariff.[3] Roosevelt would also present a model for personnel excellence in public service. Long after the crises of that period passed into history, this paradigm would stand the test of time as a superb template for those who attend the common good.

That year, with the Democratic candidate for President of the United States showing greater strength in the Midwest, West, and Northwest than in the Northeastern industrial states, the coast-to-coast swing assumed more than ordinary importance. Conventional wisdom dictated that the 21-day swing would discount any perception that FDR was not physically able to withstand the burdens of the presidency.[4]

---

[2] Michael Golay. *America 1933: The Great Depression, Lorena Hickok, Eleanor Roosevelt and the Shaping of the New Deal*, New York, NY: Simon and Schuster, 2013, pp. 11 – 17.

[3] Michael Golay. *America 1933: The Great Depression, Lorena Hickok, Eleanor Roosevelt and the Shaping of the New Deal*, New York, NY: Simon and Schuster, 2013, pp. 11 – 17.

[4] *Roosevelt Leaves On Trip To Coast*, New York, New York: New York Times, September 12, 1932, p. 1.

II - The Roosevelt Special

Nonetheless, this was a factor in planning for the excursion. Given FDR's limited mobility triggered by a 1921 bout of polio, railroads were Roosevelt's preferred mode of travel.[5] Planning centered on how best to impact the electorate through a series of speeches given at railroad stations. The campaign staff planned for the maximum impact through carefully selecting cities and towns for whistle stops.

The result was the seven-car train, known as the "Roosevelt Special." This assemblage was a complete campaign headquarters from a presidential candidate to a mimeograph machine. Beyond a particular car for the candidate were drawing room, lounge, and diner cars for the accompanying party, many of whom were correspondents and photographers.[6] The twenty-four reporters and twelve photographers occupied their time between stops by playing cards, smoking, and tapping out stories to transmitted to their newspapers by telegraph at the next stop.[7]

---

[5] Michael Golay. *America 1933: The Great Depression, Lorena Hickok, Eleanor Roosevelt and the Shaping of the New Deal*, New York, NY: Simon and Schuster, 2013, pp. 11 – 17.

[6] Staff Correspondent. *Roosevelt Leaves On Trip To Coast*, New York, New York: New York Times, September 12, 1932, p. 1.

[7] Michael Golay. *America 1933: The Great Depression, Lorena Hickok, Eleanor Roosevelt and the Shaping of the New Deal*, New York, NY: Simon and Schuster, 2013, pp. 11 – 17.

The Sunset At McCook

Roosevelt boarded the train at 11 p.m. an hour before it departed Albany, New York. Governor Roosevelt was already asleep in his private Pullman car, named Pioneer, when it left the station. Also present was a son, James, and a daughter, Anna Dall. His wife would meet the train in Arizona as she was putting two other sons in school.

Roosevelt's political objectives, laid out by his advisory team of academicians known as the "brain trust," were comparatively simple.[8] He wasn't to frighten an electorate already traumatized by the "Great Depression" but emphasize Herbert Hoover's enormous unpopularity. The result was an abundance of genial presentations replete with generalities and critiques of the incumbent's policies.

This "brain trust" included three Columbia University professors, Raymond Moley, Adolf A. Berle, Jr., and Rexford G. Tugwell.[9] Their primary responsibilities were helping write his campaign speeches and developing ideas for his presidency. Moley accompanied the president on the campaign trip.

---

[8] Alan Brinkley. *Roosevelt, Franklin Delano*, American National Biography, web site: https://doi.org/10.1093/anb/9780198606697.article.0600567, published online February 2000, accessed May 2020.
[9] Alan Brinkley. *Roosevelt, Franklin Delano*, American National Biography, web site: https://doi.org/10.1093/anb/9780198606697.article.0600567, published online February 2000, accessed May 2020.

II – The Roosevelt Special

The importance FDR placed on their contributions was symbolized in the assignment of staff in a car immediately adjoining the one occupied by FDR.[10] Occupying its stateroom were Joseph P. Kennedy, the businessperson and future father of President John F. Kennedy, and Professor Raymond Moley. Books, treatises on economics, political economy, government reports, and sundry items filled the luggage racks in this abode used for composing speeches and policy statements.

Joseph P. Kennedy was a banker was well known throughout the country. His primary responsibility was to interact with the crowd and provide outreach to political leaders.[11]

Moley assumed responsibility for gathering data and working with the candidate to help draft speeches for the trip.[12] His talent for taciturnity and ability to organize and simplify technical material was paramount.[13] He worked closely with FDR to ensure his perspective was woven into each speech while adding critical technical data. For primary addresses, Moley would call upon experts, not on the campaign

---

[10] *Roosevelt Headquarters Campaign Special*, Birmingham, Alabama: Birmingham News, September 16, 1932, p. 2.

[11] *Joseph P. Kennedy Roosevelt Adviser*, Boston Massachusetts: Boston Globe, September 24, 1932, p. 5.

[12] *Roosevelt Leaves On Trip To Coast*, New York, New York: New York Times, September 12, 1932, p. 1.

[13] *Raymond Charles Moley*, Wikipedia. web site: https://en.wikipedia.org/wiki/Raymond_Moley, accessed May 2020.

trail, for report drafts, which then were reviewed by FDR before the presentation. The speech at McCook was the result of this partnership.

After leaving Albany, the train rushed west at a steady sixty miles an hour.[14] By 1130 the next morning on September 12, the assemblage was in Bellefontaine, Ohio. This municipality domiciled about 9,500 citizens in 1930 in its location 48 miles Northwest from the state capital of Columbus. In what was to be characteristic of most stops, some 500 persons gathered for a brief platform appearance.[15]

This morning was the first of many occasions on this trip where FDR addressed a crowd standing on the rear platform of the "Roosevelt Special." He had learned in the last decade to disguise his paralysis for public purposes by wearing bulky leg braces, supporting himself with a cane and the arm of a companion, and using his hips to swing his inert legs forward.[16] The paraplegic Roosevelt would usually appear on the

---

[14] Michael Golay. *America 1933: The Great Depression, Lorena Hickok, Eleanor Roosevelt and the Shaping of the New Deal*, New York, NY: Simon and Schuster, 2013, pp. 11 – 17.

[15] Franklin Roosevelt. *Bellefontaine, Ohio - Whistlestop Remarks (speech file 494)*, September 12, 1932, web site: http://www.fdrlibrary.marist.edu/_resources/images/msf/msf00596, accessed May 2020.

[16] Alan Brinkley. *Roosevelt, Franklin Delano*, American National Biography, web site: https://doi.org/10.1093/anb/9780198606697.article.0600567, published online February 2000, accessed May 2020.

rear platform, supporting himself on a set of upright bars. These bars also served for the placement of loudspeakers.[17]

This photo illustrates the entourage as the train crossed the border between Oregon and California.

The "Roosevelt Special" Entourage (September 1932).[18]

The train journeyed to Indianapolis, Indiana, where the candidate bantered with the 500 people assembled at 2 p.m. on the 13th. Serious campaigning commenced west of the Mississippi, where press

---

[17] Michael Golay. *America 1933: The Great Depression, Lorena Hickok, Eleanor Roosevelt and the Shaping of the New Deal*, New York, NY: Simon and Schuster, 2013, pp. 11 – 17.

[18] *Photo of FDR and Campaign Entourage*, Franklin D. Roosevelt Presidential Library and Museum, web site: https://fdrlibrary.files.wordpress.com/2013/11/roosevelt-kennedy_2.jpg, accessed May 2020.

noticed that he seemed most to enjoy the prairie town whistle-stops. Often FDR found the crowds large and enthusiastic.

Each day aboard the train, the routine began almost at sunup and ended long after midnight. The Governor usually woke around 8 a.m. and was served breakfast assisted by his valet, Irvin McDuffie.[19] Soon after that, Roosevelt was looking over mail, the newspapers, and dictating letters and telegrams dispatched at the first morning stop.[20]

Speeches and schedules of the activities for the next layover were sent by Mr. Moley to the baggage car to be mimeographed and then distributed to the newspapermen and women. At each stop, there were newspaper stories dispatched and batches of telegrams received.

Daily the Governor was interviewed by the press, in the observation section, or the dining room of the car. Political leaders who constantly boarded the train for consultations. Roosevelt met them in the observation section.

---

[19] *Presidential Valets*, White House History, web site: https://www.whitehousehistory.org/presidential-valets, accessed May 2020.
[20] *Roosevelt Headquarters Campaign Special*, Birmingham, Alabama: Birmingham News, September 16, 1932, p. 2.

II - The Roosevelt Special

Always present and close to FDR was Sergeant Gus Ginnerich of the New York City police force, who served as Mr. Roosevelt's bodyguard.

By any measure, the schedule was demanding. The following chart depicts the speeches made by FDR on the campaign railroad tour before he arrived in McCook, Nebraska, on September 28.[21]

Intriguingly, the initial plan presented by the campaign on September 11 called for the stop at McCook, Nebraska, for September 28 to be a short halt without fanfare at 9:05 p.m. FDR informed the press on September 17 of the schedule change.[22]

The Governor's stop at McCook was a renewed gesture toward insurgent Republican Senators and Representatives of the Northwest who frequently voted against the policies of the Hoover Administration. Also, the Independent/Republican Senator George Norris earlier expressed support of the Roosevelt candidacy.[23]

---

[21] *Franklin D. Roosevelt Master Speech File (1898 – 1945)*, Franklin D. Roosevelt Presidential Library and Museum, web site: http://www.fdrlibrary.marist.edu/archives/collections/franklin/index.php?p= collections/findingaid&id=582, accessed May 2020.

[22] *Governor To Make Stop To See Norris*, New York, New York: New York Times, September 18, 1932, p. 33.

[23] *Governor To Make Stop To See Norris*, New York, New York: New York Times, September 18, 1932, p. 33.

The Sunset At McCook

Date of Speech (September 1932)	State	Location
12	Ohio	Bellefontaine
13	Indiana	Indianapolis
	Missouri	Jefferson City
14	Kansas	Topeka
15		Goodland
	Colorado	Limon
		Denver
16	Wyoming	Cheyenne
		Laramie
		Hanna
17	Utah	Salt Lake City
18		Ogden
		Brigham
		Cache Junction
		Pocatello
19	Montana	Butte
		Deer Lodge
20	Washington	Everett
		Seattle
21	Oregon	Portland
22	California	Dunsmuir
		Davis
		Sacramento
23		San Francisco
24		Santa Barbara
		Glendale
		Hollywood Bowl
25	Arizona	Phoenix
		Wickenburg
		Prescott
		Ash Fork
27	New Mexico	Lamy
		Las Vegas
		Ratan
	Colorado	La Junta
		Pueblo
		Colorado Springs
28	Nebraska	Benkelman
		Holdrege
		McCook

Franklin Delano Roosevelt
Political Speeches with Locations
(September 12 -28, 1932).

II – The Roosevelt Special

Crowds at each stop gathered by the rear platform of "The Pioneer."

Franklin Delano Roosevelt Speaking from "Roosevelt Special"
Goodland, Kansas, September 15, 1932.[24]

As evening approached on Tuesday, September 27, 1932, the Roosevelt entourage arrived at Colorado Springs, Colorado, at 9:00 p.m., where the candidate would spend the night at the Broadmoor Hotel.[25]

---

[24] *FDR Whistle-stopping in Goodland, Kansas – 1932*, web site: http://spiritualpilgrim.net/03_The-World-since-1900/05_Depression/05b_FDR-Takes-up-the-Challenge-2.htm, accessed June 2020.
[25] *Roosevelt Headquarters Campaign Special*, Birmingham, Alabama: Birmingham News, September 16, 1932, p. 2.

The Sunset At McCook

After a short Christmas shopping trip, the next morning by Mrs. Roosevelt, the train departed at 9:30 a.m. for Nebraska.[26]

Later as the party entered the Cornhusker State, the train stopped at the small town of Benkelman, where FDR gave a short talk and met Senator George Norris. After exchanging greeting, the "Roosevelt Special" continued the trip through Holdrege to McCook. Crowds met the candidate and his entourage in the early evening as they arrived in McCook.

On Thursday, September 29, 1932, the Knoxville (Tennessee) Republican announced that Engine Number 2825 with Engineer Clyde Scott of McCook at the controls pulled the "Roosevelt Special "on its travel over the Chicago, Burlington and Quincy railroad between Colorado and McCook in record time.[27] The run of 256 miles took five hours and five minutes, which was an hour and ten minutes faster than the speediest passenger schedule. This effort was instigated by a mistake in scheduling by campaign planners. The "Roosevelt Special" staff

---

[26] Michael Golay. *America 1933: The Great Depression, Lorena Hickok, Eleanor Roosevelt and the Shaping of the New Deal*, New York, NY: Simon and Schuster, 2013, pp. 11 - 17.
[27] *Roosevelt's Train Sets New Record For Speed*, Knoxville, Tennessee: Knoxville News-Sentinel, September 29, 1932, p. 14.

hadn't realized that, at McCook, the clock moves ahead by one hour in the change from mountain to central standard time.[28]

Engineer Scott's exemplary effort set the stage for what was to occur that evening in McCook.

[28] Federal Writers' Project of the Works Progress Administration for the State of Nebraska, *Tour 8B*, Nebraska: A Guide to the Cornhusker State, New York, New York: The Viking Press, 1939, p. 359.

III - McCook's Greatest Day

"It was McCook's greatest day. The next President of the
United States was coming. He had passed up Denver and Des Moines
and Kansas City, but little McCook was on his itinerary. For a few
hours, at least, an insignificant prairie town of fewer than eight
thousand inhabitants would hold the attention of the nation. Governor
Roosevelt was on his way to Nebraska to see George W. Norris."[1]

On Wednesday, September 28, 1932, McCook, Nebraska,
awoke to find itself in a state of excitement. On this day, they were
hailing an unprecedented visit by the Democratic candidate for
President, Franklin Delano Roosevelt. His schedule called for arrival in
the early evening by train.

The McCook Gazette, managed by local publishing legend
Harry Strunk, captured the moment on its front page.[2]

---

[1] Richard L. Neuberger and Stephen B. Kahn. *"Integrity: The Life of George
W. Norris,"* New York, New York: The Vanguard Press, 1937, pp. 298 –
302.
[2] Allen D. Strunk. *Centennial Edition (1882 – 1982),* McCook, Nebraska: The
McCook Daily Gazette, 1982.

Front Page, The McCook Daily Gazette, September 28, 1932.

That Wednesday evening, Engine Number 2825 rounded the last bend of the Chicago, Burlington, and Quincy railroad line into McCook on a record-breaking run from Colorado. Engineer Clyde Scott, a McCook native, knew that schedulers had made a potentially grievous oversight. They failed to take into account the change from mountain to central time. This mistake caused the "Roosevelt Special" to arrive almost an hour late from its original 5:10 p.m. scheduled appearance. To everyone's relief, a large crowd was there waiting patiently for the man of the hour to arrive.

III – McCook's Greatest Day

McCook in 1932 was a relatively small locality with about 7,000 persons encompassing approximately 5.38 square miles. Administratively classified as a city, it serves as the seat of Red Willow County, Nebraska.

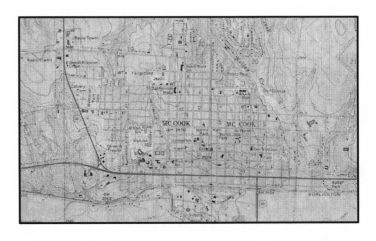

McCook, Nebraska.

The town sits in southwestern Nebraska. Kansas lies less than twenty miles to the south, and the Colorado state line is about seventy-five miles to the west. U.S. Highway 34, paralleled by the Burlington Northern Railroad, was the principal east-west route through McCook and U.S. Highway 83 stretched to North Platte.[3]

---

[3] Carl McWilliams. *McCook YMCA, Red River County, Nebraska*, U. S. Department of Interior, National Register of Historic Places, web site: https://npgallery.nps.gov/GetAsset/95fffb0a-e153-44e7-929b-038f361fd14e/, accessed May 2020.

The Sunset At McCook

Following an easterly course, to the south of the city, the Republican River is the region's most notable geographic feature.[4] The community lies approximately 2500 feet above sea-level on a gently-rising bluff which extends northward, from the bottom-land of the river. The waterway periodically floods McCook causing extensive damage.

McCook is the largest city for more than sixty miles in any direction. For this reason, it is an important agricultural center, serving farms and smaller communities throughout southwest Nebraska, northwest Kansas, and northeast Colorado.

The settlement was initially platted in 1882 and organized as a village in 1883. Brigadier General Alexander McDowell McCook, a close companion of Alexander Campbell, the first superintendent of the local division of the Burlington Railroad line, was the namesake of the town.

As McCook grew through the turn of the twentieth century, the influence of the railroad remained dominant.[5] Because of its

---

[4] Barbara Beving Long. Red Willow County Courthouse, U. S. Department of Interior, National Register of Historic Places, web site: https://npgallery.nps.gov, accessed May 2020.

[5] Carl McWilliams. *McCook YMCA, Red River County, Nebraska*, U. S. Department of Interior, National Register of Historic Places, web site:

importance as an intermediate terminal on the route to Denver, the city's early growth depended upon the Burlington railroad. In the early 20th century, seventy-five percent of McCook's labor force worked directly for the company. The remaining twenty-five percent, primarily business owners and their employees, were indirectly dependent on the railway. McCook's population between 1920 and 1930 increased more than 50 percent.[6]

It was appropriate that Franklin Roosevelt's first stop in McCook was the railroad station.

Railroad Station, McCook, Nebraska.

---

https://npgallery.nps.gov/GetAsset/95fffb0a-e153-44e7-929b-038f361fd14e/, accessed May 2020.
[6] Federal Writers' Project of the Works Progress Administration for the State of Nebraska, *Tour 8B*, Nebraska: A Guide to the Cornhusker State, New York, New York: The Viking Press, 1939, p. 358.

The Sunset At McCook

A stirring welcome greeted the "Roosevelt Special" as it pulled into the immaculate little Nebraska town that Senator George Norris called home.[7] Between two and three thousand citizens enthusiastically welcomed FDR with blowing whistles and auto horns. The candidate stopped to deliver a short greeting and made his way to the waiting motorcade.

During this Jubilee year, celebrating the 50th anniversary of its McCook's founding, civic pride was on full display. A previously scheduled "Good Roads" conference attracted a vast number of citizens from throughout the region on September 28. Governor Charles W. Bryan hosted the gathering that celebrated highway development in Nebraska. Over 5,000 persons attended during which officials from the southwestern portion of the state expressed their appreciation of the efforts to "have Nebraska completely out of the mud in two years."[8]

To make the day complete, the chamber of commerce arranged softball games, a tennis and golf tournament, horseshoe pitching contests, band concerts, a picnic, a night football game, and a dance.[9]

---

[7] Lorena A. Hickok, Associated Press Staff Writer. *"It Seems Like Old Times"* *Greets Roosevelt As Norris Boards Train,* Lincoln, Nebraska: Nebraska State Journal, *September 29, 1932, p. 4.*

[8] *Thousands Gather at McCook to Jollify Over Work Done,* Lincoln, Nebraska: Lincoln Star, September 29, 1932. P. 4.

[9] *McCook All Ready To Entertain Roosevelt,* Lincoln, Nebraska: Lincoln Journal Star, September 28, 1932, p. 10.

III – McCook's Greatest Day

In the late afternoon, enthusiasm reached a crescendo. Stores closed at 5 p.m. in both McCook and neighboring towns to allow customers and employees to greet the candidate.[10]

As FDR transferred to the motorcade, local officials put into place a security plan to ensure his safety. McCook police officers made special arrangements to guard the nominee, and Ben Danbaum, Chief Detective of the Omaha police, was on hand with four officers.[11]

Forrest Burbank, a young student from Omaha whose father owned the vehicle, drove FDR's open-air car.[12] When authorities earlier that month announced Mr. Roosevelt's visit, no suitable vehicles existed in McCook to transport the candidate from the railroad station to a rally at the Red Willow County Fairgrounds. William Bullard, the chairman of McCook's arrangements, searched the region for a suitable car and found none available. Fortunately, Mr. Burbank living in Omaha, agreed to assist the committee. On the evening of September 28, Mr. Roosevelt entered the Burbank-owned auto for a motorcade up Main Street to the Red Willow County Fairgrounds.

---

[10] *McCook Ready To Greet Roosevelt*, Lincoln, Nebraska: Lincoln Journal Star, September 28, 1932, p. 1.

[11] *McCook Ready To Greet Roosevelt*, Lincoln, Nebraska: Lincoln Journal Star, September 28, 1932, p. 1.

[12] *Democratic Leaders Are Hard Put To Find An Open Car For Roosevelt*, Omaha, Nebraska: Omaha World-Herald, September 29, 1932, p. 13.

The Sunset At McCook

The stated purpose of the visit was to honor the hometown of the United States, Senator George W. Norris. When Senator Norris returned to his hometown from Washington on September 23, he made it clear that he would not make a campaign speech nor discuss political issues with Franklin Roosevelt during their meeting on the 28th. His sole stated responsibility, endorsed by Mr. Roosevelt, was to introduce the candidate before the speech at the Fairgrounds.[13]

The motorcade began their journey up Main Street at about 6 p.m. Their destination was about one mile away at the Red Willow County Fairgrounds on the outskirts of the city. Senator Norris sat with the candidate in the back of the open car, and together they greeted the throngs of citizens that lined the route.

The first segment of the parade passed through the commercial district, rising on Main Street to the residential area. After the Senator died in the 1940s, city fathers renamed the road in his honor.

---

[13] *Norris Glad To Be Home.* Lincoln, Nebraska: Lincoln Journal Star, September 23, 1932, p. 7.

III – McCook's Greatest Day

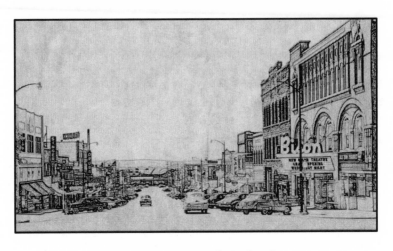

Main Street, McCook, Nebraska.

An estimated 4,000 cheering spectators lined the streets as FDR, and Senator Norris passed.[14] While riding up the hill, the Nebraska statesman probably made small talk while pointing outbuildings of particular significance to him. Two structures held of specific importance. There was Floyd Hagenberger's barbershop, where he would regularly get a morning shave. Another location that held a special place in his heart was the real estate office of Carl Marsh. The Senator would make his way almost daily to converse with anyone who dropped in.[15]

---

[14] Lorena Hickok. *It Seems Like Old Times...Greets Roosevelt As Norris Boards Train*, Lincoln, Nebraska: Nebraska State Journal, September 29, 1932, p. 4.
[15] *Senator George W. Norris*, Chicago, Illinois: Time Magazine, Volume XXIX, January 11, 1937, p. 16.

The Sunset At McCook

Almost a half-mile up the hill on Main Street, the party entered a residential area of quiet shady streets. A United States flag on a pole signaled the entrance to this suburban community.

Flagpole, Main Street, McCook, Nebraska.

To the press corps accompanying the convoy, McCook appeared as a prosperous-looking town. Lawns looked fresh and green, houses seemed freshly painted, and in this residential neighborhood, the parade passed newly constructed bungalows.[16] Flags fluttered for the occasion from porches, and along the way, families waved their hands and shouted, "Hello Frank, good luck governor."

---

[16] Lorena Hickok. *It Seems Like Old Times…Greets Roosevelt As Norris Boards Train*, Lincoln, Nebraska: Nebraska State Journal, September 29, 1932, p. 4.

III - McCook's Greatest Day

Several blocks into this neighborhood, the party passed Senator Norris' modest two-story stucco home where he still cut the lawn and trimmed the bushes. Norris purchased the house in 1899, from a railroad superintendent.[17]

About one mile after leaving the railroad station, the party turned left on West O Street for the final leg into the Fairgrounds. Continuing in a residential community for just over a quarter mile Roosevelt, Norris, and their party arrived at the Red Willow County Fairgrounds at a little past 6 p.m.

Red Willow County Fairgrounds in 1934, McCook, Nebraska.[18]

---

[17] James Denney. *Centennial Year For Norris*, Omaha, Nebraska: Omaha World-Herald, May 14, 1961, p. 102.

[18] *County Fairgrounds Improvement, McCook (1934),* History Nebraska, Nebraska State Historical Society, web site: https://nebraskahistory.pastperfectonline.com/photo/E714ECE4-565B-4311-B6DA-750102729214, accessed June 2020.

The Sunset At McCook

As the party entered the grandstand area, bands from twelve nearby towns, massed in a group of 400 musicians, greeted the nominee with a delivery of the Double Eagle March.[19]

The grandstand sat only 4,500 of the estimated crowd of 16,000. The race track at the seat of the stands served as standing room for the overflow, which spilled over several acres of the fairground. Nearly three times the town's population was present. They listened attentively to hear what was billed, at the request of Senator Norris, a non-political speech.

Floodlights lit the fairgrounds in the fading daylight. Their beams caught and illuminated an American flag that fluttered from a pole in the dusty track.[20] Loudspeakers stood beside the open cars so that all could hear. A national radio audience listened from microphones placed prominently before the candidate. Mrs. Roosevelt, her daughter, Mrs. Curtis Doll, and daughter-in-law Mrs. James Roosevelt sat on a low fence near the track.[21]

---

[19] *Senator Norris To Welcome Demo Chief To State*, Lincoln, Nebraska: The Lincoln Star, September 28, 1932, p. 1.

[20] Lorena Hickok. *It Seems Like Old Times...Greets Roosevelt As Norris Boards Train*, Lincoln, Nebraska: Nebraska State Journal, September 29, 1932, p. 4.

[21] Associated Press, *McCook Ready To Greet Roosevelt*, Lincoln, Nebraska: Lincoln Journal Star, September 28, 1932, p. 1.

III - McCook's Greatest Day

Security staff assisted Franklin Delano Roosevelt to stand below the grandstand where he could be supported by his car.

The red sun dropped below the open horizon at 6:30 p.m. and dusk fell.[22]

A Sunset At McCook (2017),
Red Willow County Fairgrounds,
McCook, Nebraska.[23]

---

[22] *When did the sun set at McCook Nebraska on September 28, 1932?*, Google.com, Web site:
https://www.google.com/search?q=when+was+sunset+at+mccook+nebraska+on+september+28+1932&rlz=1C5CHFA_enUS509US509&oq=when+was+sunset+at+mccook+nebraska+on+september+28+1932&aqs=chrome..69i57.12082j0j4&sourceid=chrome&ie=UTF-8, accessed June 2020.
[23] *Red Willow County Fair (July 2017)*, Facebook.com, web site:
https://www.facebook.com/171231839603565/photos/a.532180466842032/1515735105153225, accessed June 2020.

The Sunset At McCook

The stage was set for one of the most noteworthy but unheralded speeches in the rhetorical history of Franklin Delano Roosevelt.

IV – An Inquiry Into True Greatness In A Public Official

The remarks presented by Franklin Roosevelt that afternoon were composed hurriedly on a train during a demanding campaign trip that stretched over many weeks. The comments made national newspapers the next day and quickly forgotten in subsequent news cycles. Academic researchers do not classify the words as being noteworthy. Moreover, the Franklin Delano Roosevelt Presidential Library does not include a transcript in its cataloged repository of speeches. The title ascribed by staff for the file symbolizes its relative importance, *McCook, Nebraska - Extemporaneous Remarks (Speech File 539), September 28, 1932.*[1]

Newspaper articles the next day described the McCook speech as one limited to honoring Senator George Norris. Its wording reflected Nebraska's friendly demeanor.

Despite its humble roots, these almost 1,000 words, delivered by Franklin Roosevelt in about 8 minutes, provide a well-defined model for those who seek excellence in public service. While praising in 36 sentences Senator Norris' sincerity of purpose, the oration is an inquiry

---

[1] *Franklin D. Roosevelt, Master Speech File, 1898-1945*, Franklin D. Roosevelt Presidential Library & Museum, web site: http://www.fdrlibrary.marist.edu/_resources/images/msf/msf000551, accessed June 2020.

into what constitutes true greatness in a public official.[2] Its central message reveals that it is not temporary acclaim or ephemeral popularity, which matters. Integrity, unselfishness, courage, and Consistency are the lasting qualities of public service that endure through time.[3]

Mr. Roosevelt's rhetorical fluency enhanced its impact on the crowd.[4] As an accomplished orator, he communicated the subtle range of his feelings in a manner that imparted directness and sincerity to his listeners.[5] He talked to, not at the American people. Amid the Great Depression, he appeared to offer solutions to the Midwest farmer's woes. Using easily understood phrases, FDR presented an image of himself as a leader of vision and action. Roosevelt worked his way into their hearts, speaking as a friend to the men and women of Nebraska. His style involved a smile, a gesture, and a capacity for grave concern. In response, the audience of almost 20,000 appeared to accept him as their companion.

---

[2] Richard L. Neuberger and Stephen B. Kahn. *"Integrity: The Life of George W. Norris,"* New York, New York: The Vanguard Press, 1937, pp. 298 – 302.

[3] Ibid.

[4] Halford R. Ryan. *Franklin D. Roosevelt's Rhetorical Presidency*, New York, New York: Greenwood Press, 1988, p. 13.

[5] Ibid.

IV - An Inquiry Into True Greatness In A Public Official

Political acumen guided Roosevelt's thoughts. Although nominally a Republican, Senator Norris endorsed the Democrat for the Presidency in the 1932 presidential campaign. Sensing an opportunity, Roosevelt wanted to use this support to attract other similarly-minded Republicans to his side. However, Franklin Roosevelt never expressed such admiration in public about the personal qualities of another living political leader.[6]

Upon arrival, the candidate left the automobile and stood while supported by its side door. The crowd, both in the grandstand and in the racing track, held in an amphitheater around FDR. The speaking began at 6:30 p.m. and continued through the sunset until darkness fell.

The crowd first listened to Senator Norris as he commenced the event.[7] This snapshot taken that day by newspaper photographers captures the moment the Senator introduced Mr. Roosevelt.

---

[6] Thomas P. Wolf, William D. Pederson, and Byron W. Daynes. *Franklin D. Roosevelt and Congress: The New Deal and Its Aftermath Volume II*, Armonk, New York: M. E. Sharpe, 2001, p. 8.
[7] *Norris Introduces Roosevelt at McCook*, Omaha World-Herald, September 29, 1932, p. 1

The Sunset At McCook

Presidential Candidate Franklin Delano Roosevelt
Being introduced by the United States Senator George W. Norris
At the Red Willow County Fairgrounds,
McCook, Nebraska, September 28, 1932
(Source: Thompson Photo Archives)

The introduction of Franklin Roosevelt was the first speech delivered by Norris following his announcement of support for the Democratic Presidential nominee. The McCook resident used the address to tell his hometown crowd that FDR was an exceptional friend of the common man.[8]

Just as Senator Norris was in the midst of his address praising Governor Roosevelt, the National Broadcasting Company's suspended

---

[8] *Norris Introduces Roosevelt at McCook*, Omaha World-Herald, September 29, 1932, p. 1.

its radio coverage of the event. This decision was due to NBC resuming its regular broadcasting schedule because of the late arrival of the "Roosevelt Special" in McCook.[9] Thus, the nation never heard FDR's speech.

In the sections that follow, text boxes highlight the script of the speech grouped by theme in the order spoken by Franklin Roosevelt. A short narrative follows clarifying in more detail the topics raised by the candidate. The design of the font is similar to that used by newspapers of the 1930s.

> **I am happy to be with you progressive citizens of Nebraska today.**
>
> **You are progressive, not alone by long practice, but equally by a deep-seated intuitive understanding.**
>
> **Your hearts and minds understand the true meaning of the word humanitarian and support constant progress in behalf of the prosperity and the happiness of our people.**

Roosevelt began the speech with a greeting to the audience as "progressives." The term, as used at that time, meant a political ideology

---

[9] Omaha World-Herald. *Halt Broadcast of McCook Program*, Omaha, Nebraska: Omaha World-Herald Newspaper, September 29, 1932, p. 2.

that favored rational governmental action to improve society.[10] The
philosophy arose in response to industrialism and dominated American
politics from the 1890s to the 1920s. Being called a progressive in the
1930s was a kindly noncontroversial refrain.

> I believe too that the great majority of thinking
> people throughout the nation have come to
> realize that this is the true basic reason for your
> support of your great progressive statesman,
> Senator Norris.
>
> This support, even in his independent political
> action, demands with increasing respect and
> sympathy the admiration of every patriotic citizen
> in the East as well as in the West.

By 1932, his legislative skills, integrity, honesty, and positive
legislative accomplishments earned George William Norris (1861–
1944) a stellar reputation for political courage.[11] After his death,
numerous nationwide polls ranked Norris as one of the greatest senators
in American history. Biographers remark that the Nebraskan served his
country and its people well through a long and honorable public career.

---

[10] *The Progressive Era*, Lumen: Boundless U.S. History, web site,
https://courses.lumenlearning.org, accessed June 2020.
[11] Wayne S. Cole. *Norris, George William*, American National Biography,
web site: https://doi.org/10.1093/anb/9780198606697.article.0600476,
accessed June 2020.

IV – An Inquiry Into True Greatness In A Public Official

> In our long national history we have seen in every decade the rise of public servants to positions of great power and acclaim.
>
> In my studies of our history I have always been deeply interested in the fact that the appraisal of the greatness of statesmen by their contemporaries has often been completely reversed by a later verdict.
>
> If you will take even the history of any one State during a given ten years you will find a de facto leadership and a temporary acclaim for many political leaders whose very names are wholly forgotten a generation later.
>
> We should remember that the ultimate analysis of history asks the answer to questions which are not concerned so much with what you and I, in these modern days, call ballyhoo, or headlines, as they are with much simpler fundamentals.

Over the years, determining the relative quality and impact of service by individual United States Senators to their country has been the subject of numerous studies and polls. Since there are no standardized and easily quantifiable criteria, the results are often partisan, reflecting contemporary societal values. Thus, these efforts have little value for serious researchers.

For example, in 1986, the Siena College Research Institute located in Loudonville, New York, conducted a random sample of 400

college historians and political scientists. More than 110 responded.[12]
The pollsters ranked Senators based on leadership ability, political
leadership, luck, imagination, intelligence, ability to compromise,
integrity, importance to Senate, value to the country, and legislative
creativity. Henry Clay of Kentucky achieved the ranking of the nation's
most excellent Senator. George W. Norris placed the fifth most
exceptional United States Senator of all time.

Another more politically visible effort occurred in the mid-
1950s. The future President John F. Kennedy, as Senator from
Massachusetts, chaired a Senate select committee to determine the best
senators in American history. This initiative became politically-charged
even though the group sought the advice of historians in ascertaining
criteria and seeking counsel.[13] The committee, after much wrangling,
settled on several rules. First, nominees should be distinguished for acts
of statesmanship transcending State and party lines. Second, the
selection was not based on their services while in other offices. Finally,
their diplomacy could include leadership in political thought and
constitutional interpretation as well as legislation. This process resulted
in the selection of Senator Norris as one of the most exceptional
Senators in United States Senate history. However, a single committee

---

[12] *Henry Clay is Rated Greatest U.S. Senator*, New York, New York: New York Times, May 5, 1986, p. 35.
[13] John T. Shaw. *When John F. Kennedy Judged the Senate's Greats*, History News Network, web site: historynewsnetwork.org, accessed June 2020.

member successfully vetoed his nomination due to personal animosity. This act cast doubt on the legitimacy of the process.

Presidential Candidate Franklin Delano Roosevelt delivering remarks
While standing next to U.S. Senator George W. Norris
At Red Willow County Fairgrounds,
McCook, Nebraska, September 28, 1932
(Source: Thompson Photo Archives)

Roosevelt then proposed that four qualities establish a public servant's relative consequence. Definitions and quoted from knowledgeable sources reflect on their connotation.

History asks: "Did the man have integrity?"

- Definition: "Firm adherence to a code of especially moral or artistic values."[14]

- Quote: "Integrity results from the relentless pursuit of honesty at all times."[15]

- Quote: "You are already of consequence in the world if you are known as a man of strict integrity."[16]

- Quote: "Nothing discloses real character like the use of power. It is easy for the weak to be gentle. Most people can bear adversity. But if you wish to know what a man is, give him power. This challenge is the supreme test."[17]

---

[14] *Integrity*. Merriam-Webster Dictionary, web site: www.merriam-webster.com/dictionary/integrity, accessed May 2020.
[15] *Wise Integrity Quotes*, web site: wiseoldsayings.com/integrity-quotes, accessed May 2020.
[16] Greenville Kiesier. Ibid.
[17] Robert Green Ingersoll. *Selections from his Oratory and Writings*, web site: https://bartleby.com/400/prose/1827.html, accessed May 2020.

IV – An Inquiry Into True Greatness In A Public Official

> **"Did the man have unselfishness?"**

- Definition: "The quality of not putting yourself first but being willing to give your time or money etc. for others."[18]

- Quote: "Only a life lived for others is a life worth living."[19]

- Quote: "When no one is selfless in a relationship, there is war. When one is selfless, there is peace. When both are selfless, there is joy."[20]

- Quote: "Give me a few men and women who are pure and selfless, and I shall shake the world."[21]

---

[18] *Unselfishness*, Vocabulary.com, web site: www.vocabulary.com/dictionary/unselfishness, accessed May 2020.
[19] Albert Einstein. *Wise Old Sayings*, web site: wiseoldsayings.com/selfless-quotes/, accessed May 2020.
[20] Royce White. *Wise Old Sayings*, web site: wiseoldsayings.com/selfless-quotes/, accessed May 2020.
[21] Swami Vivekananda. *Wise Old Sayings*, web site: wiseoldsayings.com/selfless-quotes/, accessed May 2020.

> ## "Did the man have courage?"

- Definition: "Mental or moral strength to venture, persevere, and withstand danger, fear, or difficulty."[22]

- Quote: "It is better for men to hate you are than to be loved for what you are not."[23]

- Quote: Do what you can, with what you have, where you are."[24]

- Quote: "Courage is what it takes to stand up and speak; courage is also what it takes to sit down and listen."[25]

---

[22] *Courage.* Merriam-Webster Dictionary, web site: www.merriam-webster.com/dictionary/courage, accessed May 2020.

[23] Andre Gide. *Courage*, Fearlessmotivation.com, web site: fearlessmotivation.com/2015/12/18/17-of-the-most-powerful-notes-on-courage/, accessed May 2020.

[24] Theodore Roosevelt. *Courage*, Fearlessmotivation.com, web site: fearlessmotivation.com/2015/12/18/17-of-the-most-powerful-notes-on-courage/, accessed May 2020.

[25] Winston Churchill. *Courage*, Fearlessmotivation.com, web site: fearlessmotivation.com/2015/12/18/17-of-the-most-powerful-notes-on-courage/, accessed May 2020.

> ## "Did the man have consistency?"

- Definition: "Firmness of constitution or character."[26]

- Quote: "I hope that I shall possess firmness and virtue enough to maintain what I consider the most enviable of all titles, the character of an honest man."[27]

- Quote: "Consistency leads to habits. Habits mold the actions we take every day. Action leads to success."[28]

- Quote: "Consistency embodies that work whose whole and detail are suitable for the occasion. It arises from circumstance, custom, and nature."[29]

---

[26] *Consistency*. Merriam-Webster Dictionary, web site: www.merriam-webster.com/dictionary/consistency, accessed May 2020.

[27] George Washington. *Conversation with Alexander Hamilton, Thursday, August 28, 1788*, Fred W. Smith National Library for the Study of George Washington, web site: https://www.mountvernon.org/library/digitalhistory/quotes/, accessed May 2020.

[28] Srdjan Coric. *Consistency: The Key to Success*, web site: https://medium.com/launch-school/consistency-the-key-to-success, published on October 24, 2017, accessed May 2020.

[29] Joseph Gwilt. *The Architecture of Marcus Vitruvius in Ten Books*, London. England: Priestley and Weale Publishers, 1826, p. 12.

The Sunset At McCook

> And if the individual under the scrutiny of the historic microscope measured up to an affirmative answer to these questions then history has set him down as great indeed in the pages of all the years to come.

- Quote: "Some are born great, some achieve greatness, and some have greatness thrust upon them."[30]

---

[30] William Shakespeare. *Twelfth Night, Act 2 Scene 5*, Brainy Quotes, web page: https://www.brainyquote.com/quotes/william_shakespeare_101484, accessed June 2020.

Franklin Roosevelt Speaking At Red Willow Fairgrounds,
McCook, Nebraska, on September 28, 1932.
(Source: Thompson Photo Archives)

At that point, Governor Roosevelt paused and looked over thousands
of engaged faces of the crowd. At this juncture, the staccato of the telegraph
keys could be heard from the press table as FDR prepared to deliver his crucial
message.[31]

---

[31] Richard L. Neuberger and Stephen B. Kahn. *"Integrity: The Life of George
W. Norris,"* New York, New York: The Vanguard Press, 1937, pp. 298 –
302.

> There are few statesmen in America today who so definitely and clearly measure up to affirmative to the four questions as does the senior Senator from Nebraska. In his rare case, history has already written the verdict.

As FDR turned in acknowledgment toward the Senator, the hometown crowd burst into a roar of agreement.[32] The reporters knowingly grinned at Senator Norris for the staff they had copies of the speech in front of them. For the next few minutes, while torrents of cheers rose through the autumn haze, Roosevelt delivered an unprecedented tribute to the senior Senator from Nebraska.

---

[32] Richard L. Neuberger and Stephen B. Kahn. *"Integrity: The Life of George W. Norris,"* New York, New York: The Vanguard Press, 1937, pp. 298 – 302.

Not you alone in Nebraska, but we in every part of the nation, give full recognition to his integrity, to his unselfishness, to his courage and to his consistency. He stands forth -whether we agree with him on all the little details or not – he stands forth as the very perfect, gentle knight of American progressive ideals.

I am hoping that at this moment thousands of boys and girls – thousands of first voters – are listening to my words, for I should like them to give some thought and some study to the very remarkable public service of the man in whose home town I now stand.

- Biographical Quote: "Some men who rise as he rose to turn out to be men of one battle and no more. Unaffected by the lures and pressures of Washington, Norris remained to the end the same Norris."[33]

- Biographical Quote: "He looked no Hercules! Norris' friends, to say Nothing of his crowding enemies, disputed whether he was even great. We found him when we came at last to know him, a man without a front. He was plain George Norris, taking the back seat in any crowd with a modesty not put on. Not till, in his talk, he came to some wrong weighing upon his mind, did

---

[33] Walter Locke. *George W. Norris, Independent*, The Antioch Review, Summer, 1945, Vol. 5, No. 2 (Summer, 1945), pp. 274-284 Web site: http://www.jstor.com/stable/4609081, accessed June 2020.

the power that was in him show itself. Then would come a certain outward thrust of the jaw which told you this man, for all his mildness, was dangerous. His words were soft. Seldom did anger rule his tongue. He spoke kindly of the men he had to fight and felt as kindly as he spoke. But of the fighting man, that unconscious thrust of jaw spoke louder than his words."[34]

> I should like them to read of his able and heroic fight on behalf of the average citizen which he has made during his long and honorable career. I should like them to know that sometimes he has made this fight with his party, and sometimes – as now – against the leader of his party.

In 1931 Senator Norris said he was not even sure what Franklin D. Roosevelt of New York looked like since he had never met the Governor.[35] Norris did not agree with Roosevelt on all issues. Nevertheless, he considered the New Yorker the best hope for those seeking progressive reforms. Even before the Democratic national convention in 1932, Nebraska's senior Senator declared he would support Roosevelt. This decision helped to convince other independent Republicans to support Roosevelt's candidacy.

---

[34] Walter Locke. *George W. Norris, Independent*, The Antioch Review, Summer, 1945, Vol. 5, No. 2 (Summer, 1945), pp. 274-284 Web site: http://www.jstor.com/stable/4609081, accessed June 2020.
[35] Richard L. Neuberger and Stephen B. Kahn. *"Integrity: The Life of George W. Norris,"* New York, New York: The Vanguard Press, 1937, pp. 298 – 302.

IV - An Inquiry Into True Greatness In A Public Official

> I should like them to know that always he has been thinking of the rights and the welfare of the average citizen, of the farmer, the laborer, the small business man – yes, and of the rights and the welfare of those who have been born to or have acquired greater wealth.
>
> But especially it has been an unselfish fight, and directed to the fact that it is the little fellow who has the fewest friends in high places, and that too often it is the little fellow who has been forgotten by his government.

- Biographical Quote: "In the field of domestic legislative policy, the Senator's sympathies were always with the little people farmers, workers, and small businessmen."[36]

- Biographical Quote: "Passionate intensity dominated his political life as he fought against "special interests," "Wall Street," "monopoly," and "the power trust."[37]

---

[36] David Fellman. *The Liberalism of Senator Norris*, The American Political Science Review , Feb., 1946, Vol. 40, No. 1 (Feb., 1946), p. 43, web site: http://www.jstor.com/stable/1949944, accessed June 2020.
[37] George Norris. *The Spider Web of Wall Street*, Washington, D.C.: The Congressional Record, 72nd Congress, 2nd Session, Volume 76, Part T pp. 4769 – 4780.

- Biographical Quote: "When he says that he is for the Common Man and against the Special Interests, it takes a double-doubting Thomas to disbelieve him, for his record backs him up on every point."[38]

- Biographical Quote: "For George W. Norris, the primary problem for American democracy was whether all the people or the powerful few would control the government. This fundamental concern that the oligarchical concentration of political control would inevitably result in economic oppression re-enforced an almost religious belief in the virtue and wisdom of the common man."[39]

> I have spoken of his consistency – and by this I mean a consistency in the great things of life; a consistency which has held through the years, through success and adversity towards a goal that overlooks the pettiness and the jealousies of politics as we use politics in the wrong and narrower sense.

[38] *R.F.D. to F.D.R.*, Chicago, Illinois: Time Magazine, Volume XXI, Number 2, January 11, 1937, p. 18.
[39] Norman L. Zucker, *George W. Norris: Gentle Knight of American Democracy,* Urbana: University of Illinois Press, 1966), 30, web site: http://www.questia.com/read/65865771/george-w-norris-gentle-knight-of-american-democracy, accessed, June 2020.

- Biographical Quote: "A man who did not love people, the people as they are, could never have walked as straight before them as did he. When George thought, as he was often urged to do, of the autobiography which he might write, his mind turned from the times and events in which he had played. Norris turned to the boyhood and youth out of which this career of his had grown. That, to him, was the decisive thing. The war in the Senate on graft and privilege was born in the struggle on that old Ohio farm. The parliamentary point of order in the Senate that saved Muscle Shoals was born in the country, debating society of his youthful days. Norris, to the end, was what he was there on that farm, the common man, a lover, and defender of the common man."[40]

> During this campaign, as the Senator knows, I have stressed the fact that my quarrel is not with the millions of splendid men and woman who in the past have called themselves Republicans, but that my battle is against certain forces now in the control of the leadership of the Republican party, who have forgotten the principles in which that party was founded and have become representative of a selfish few, who put personal interests above national good.

---

[40] Walter Locke. *George W. Norris, Independent*, The Antioch Review, Summer, 1945, Vol. 5, No. 2 (Summer, 1945), pp. 274-284 Web site: http://www.jstor.com/stable/4609081, accessed June 2020.

The Sunset At McCook

- Biographical Quote: "By that time, the tide of revolt which was to land him in the Senate had begun to rise in his party. Eastern interests controlled the party. Thence came its campaign funds and the free railroad tickets on which the party leaders, state and county, rode—the organization submitted to this control. The rank-and-file Republicans, to defend their obvious interests, had to oppose these controls—that meant revolt within the party. To the free-pass-riding Republican, this was treason, but to the mass of Nebraska voters, it was common sense. They revolted to such effect that in 1907 a Republican state convention routed the party machine, wrote its platform, and smashed the machine slate of candidates."[41]

- Biographical Quote: "The defiance by Senator Norris of the party machine was thus popular with the Nebraska people, though never with the party bosses. The farm depression following the First World War did not wait for '29. While the business boom of the Harding-Coolidge days swept up and on, the farmers slid steadily into insolvency. Republican presidents vetoed the farm relief bills, which Norris helped push through Congress. His opposition to these Republican presidents was pleasing to suffering Nebraskan Republicans, save only the

---

[41] Ibid.

professional party regulars. Norris became the symbol of bold and able resistance to the powers which had so long exploited the state. Farmers began, at last, to see how the tariffs imposed by the party for which they had voted them. They applauded Norris' tariff insurgency. They approved him so decided that they did in 1936 the amazing, unprecedented thing of electing him, though unsupported by any party organization, as an independent candidate. Norris served, from the start of his career, the interests of the people. In supporting the insurgent Norris, the people of Nebraska had served their own proper economic needs and interests. And the people, with their direct primary, ruled."[42]

---

[42] Walter Locke. *George W. Norris, Independent*, The Antioch Review, Summer, 1945, Vol. 5, No. 2 (Summer, 1945), pp. 274-284 Web site: http://www.jstor.com/stable/4609081, accessed June 2020.

That is why I rejoice in and approve the statement that Senator Norris is "a better Republican than President Hoover.

To those who say that Senator Norris has been no respecter of parties, I would suggest something more important "The forces of evil are far less respecters of parties."

Those bankers and brokers who, in order to obtain a commission, will willingly deceive an investing public into buying worthless domestic or foreign bonds, are no respecter of party. A conscienceless power trust seeking to change the home owner, the small manufacturer, the little business man, all the traffic will bear, is no respecter of parties.

These men and these organizations seek to fatten themselves by the use of the kind of party regularity – whether it be Republican of Democratic – which can best be purchased to serve them.

Theirs is the type of bad citizenship which cries the loudest against public servants like Senator Norris, who is consistent, unselfish, courageous and can't be bought.

- Biographical Quote: "The success of Nebraska's great Senator was all the more remarkable when viewed in the light of the unorthodoxy of his methods. He belonged to no church and never went through pietistic motions to secure the vote of warm religionists. The only religion he ever acknowledged was a general faith in the brotherhood of man. He refused to be intimidated by pressure groups, the *enfants terribles* of American politics, and often fought them tooth and nail. He did not play the patronage game, supposedly so essential for political success. He cheerfully fought some of the most powerful men in American life. He paid no attention to party allegiance and had the party machine on his stubborn neck most of the time. He put on none of the airs of the elder statesman, even when he became an authentic member of the genus. He always preferred to follow what he thought were the dictates of his conscience, which is often a poison for democratic politicians."[43]

These are the lineal descendants of the men and the organizations who called Jefferson a "radical"; who called Jackson a "demagogue"; who called Lincoln a "crack-pot idealist"; who called Theodore Roosevelt a "wild man"; who called Woodrow Wilson an "impractical idealist."

Senator Norris, I go along with you because it is my honest belief that you follow in their footsteps - radical like Jackson, idealist like Lincoln, wild like Theodore Roosevelt, theorist like Wilson – dare to be all of these, as you have in bygone years.

---

[43] Walter Locke. *George W. Norris, Independent,* The Antioch Review, Summer, 1945, Vol. 5, No. 2 (Summer, 1945), pp. 274-284 Web site: http://www.jstor.com/stable/4609081, accessed June 2020.

The Political Legacy of Thomas Jefferson (1743–1826).

- "Though undeniably a great man and a giant among the Founding Fathers, Jefferson has more difficulty qualifying as a great President. Jack-of-all-trades and master of many, he comes close to the 18th century ideal of a universal genius. In some respects, he could more easily rank among the five greatest Americans of all time than among the five greatest Presidents."[44]

- Jefferson was a superb political organizer and a master in leading Congress. However, this led to the development of a unique spoils system.

- He formed a new political party, infusing it with a more refreshing concept of democracy, strengthened the two-term tradition, stood up to the Tripolitan pirates, and promoted the exploration of the West through the Lewis and Clark Expedition.

- As President, he justified divergent conceptions of executive power. Jefferson jettisoned strict construction when he noticed that threats evolved to the nation's vital interests. Self-

---

[44] Thomas A Bailey. *Presidential Greatness: The Image and the Man from George Washington to the Present*, New York, New York: Appleton Century, 1966, p. 272.

preservation took precedence over the constitutional limitations that he carefully observed in peacetime.[45]

- Thomas Jefferson eloquently articulated fundamental tensions in Americans' understanding of the people's power. Where an enlightened people determined their destiny, Jefferson promised, there was no necessary or inevitable conflict between private rights and the public good.

The Political Legacy of Andrew Jackson (1767– 1845)

- "Andrew Jackson, in my judgment, is overrated as President and does not belong in the highest echelon, where the Schlesinger experts at first put him. They later dropped him to the top of the Near Greats. He should rate not better than High Average if that."[46]

- "Much depends on one's tests and their relevancy. Jackson was a great national hero, a great popular leader, a great party catalyst, and a great public figure. He had a powerful impact on the

---

[45] Peter Onuf. *Thomas Jefferson: Impact and Legacy*, Miller Center, University of Virginia, Web site: https://millercenter.org/president/jefferson/impact-and-legacy, accessed June 2020.
[46] Thomas A Bailey. *Presidential Greatness: The Image and the Man from George Washington to the Present*, New York, New York: Appleton Century, 1966, p. 277.

presidential office and on his times. However, not all of the controversy and had-cracking were for the best."[47]

- "He was a great American in many respects, especially when we consider his educational and cultural limitations, but hardly a great President."[48]

- "Andrew Jackson left a permanent imprint upon American politics and the Presidency. Within eight years, he melded the amorphous coalition of personal followers who had elected him into the country's most durable and successful political party, an electoral machine whose organization and discipline would serve as a model for all others. The Democratic party was Jackson's child; the national two-party system was his legacy."[49]

- "Jackson was both a fiery patriot and a strident partisan. Regarding the national Union as indivisible and perpetual, he denounced nullification and secession. Some praise his strength and audacity; others see him as vengeful and self-obsessed. To admirers, he stands as a shining symbol of American accomplishment, the ultimate individualist and democrat. To

---

[47] Ibid.

[48] Ibid.

[49] Daniel Feller. *Andrew Jackson: Impact and Legacy*, Miller Center, University of Virginia, Web site: https://millercenter.org/president/jackson/impact-and-legacy, accessed June 2020.

detractors, he appears an incipient tyrant, the closest we have yet come to an American Caesar."[50]

The Political Legacy of Abraham Lincoln (1809 – 1865).

- "So many layers of worship, idolatry, and mythology cling to the homely frame of Abraham Lincoln that one is puzzled to know how much is left when they are all chipped away. He was unquestionably one of the strongest Presidents. He had to become one, despite his modest nature, to preserve the Union. The path to glory lay in simply doing what plain duty forced upon him. His career beautifully illustrates the axiom that Nothing succeeds like success, no matter how much fumbling there may be on the road to victory."[51]

- "In 1982, forty-nine historians and political scientists were asked by the Chicago Tribune to rate all the Presidents through Jimmy Carter in five categories: leadership qualities, accomplishments/crisis management, political skills, appointments, and character/integrity. At the top of the list stood Abraham Lincoln. Franklin Roosevelt, George Washington, Theodore Roosevelt, Thomas Jefferson, Andrew

---

[50] Ibid.
[51] Thomas A Bailey. *Presidential Greatness: The Image and the Man from George Washington to the Present*, New York, New York: Appleton Century, 1966, p. 291.

Jackson, Woodrow Wilson, and Harry Truman followed him. None of these other Presidents exceeded Lincoln in any category according to the rating scale. Roosevelt fell into second place because he did not measure up to Lincoln in character. Washington, close behind, ranked third because of his lesser political skills. It is the general opinion of pollsters, moreover, that the average American would probably put Lincoln at the top as well. In other words, the judgment of historians and the public tells us that Abraham Lincoln was the nation's greatest President by every measure applied."[52]

- "The most lasting accomplishments attributed to Lincoln are the preservation of the Union, the explanation of democracy, and the death of slavery, all accomplished by how he handled the crisis that most certainly would have ended differently with a lesser man in office. His great achievement, historians tell us, was his ability to energize and mobilize the nation by appealing to its best ideals while acting "with malice towards none" in the pursuit of a more perfect, more just, and more enduring Union. No President in American history ever faced a more significant crisis, and no President ever accomplished as much."[53]

---

[52] Michael Burlingame. *Abraham Lincoln: Impact and Legacy*, Miller Center, University of Virginia, Web site: https://millercenter.org/president/lincoln/impact-and-legacy, accessed June 2020.
[53] Ibid.

IV - An Inquiry Into True Greatness In A Public Official

- "Lincoln's reputation lies perhaps not so much in what he did as in what he endured. He remains a classic symbol of Union, democracy and presidential presence in a time of crisis. We can hardly deny him a place somewhere among the Greats, though he may not have been a super-great."[54]

The Political Legacy of Theodore Roosevelt (1858 – 1919).

- "Theodore Roosevelt is widely regarded as the first modern President of the United States. The stature and influence that the office has today began to develop with T.R. Throughout the second half of the 1800s; Congress had been the most powerful branch of government. And although the Presidency began to amass more power during the 1880s, Roosevelt completed the transition to a strong, effective executive. He made the President, rather than the political parties or Congress, the center of American politics. Roosevelt did this through the force of his personality and aggressive executive action. He thought that the President had the right to use all powers unless statutes denied him. He believed that as President, he had a unique relationship with and responsibility to the people, and therefore wanted to challenge prevailing notions of limited

---

[54] Thomas A Bailey. *Presidential Greatness: The Image and the Man from George Washington to the Present*, New York, New York: Appleton Century, 1966, p. 293.

government and individualism; government, he maintained, should serve as an agent of reform for the people."[55]

- "Roosevelt was a great personality, a great activist, a great preacher of the moralities, a great conversationalist, a great showman. He dominated his era as he dominated conversations. Sometimes people wondered whether they had an administration or a circus. He was a great egoist, a great self-glorifier, a great exhibitionist, a great headline-catcher, so much that some critics felt he had degraded the high office. But the masses loved him; he proved to be a popular idol a great vote-getter. A consummate politician, he was also a great opportunist and withal a great leader. Yet, on balance, Roosevelt felt short of being a Grade-A President, at best he was B plus, or a Near Great, as the experts have decreed."[56]

- "In terms of presidential style, Roosevelt introduced "charisma" into the political equation. He had a strong rapport with the public, and he understood how to use the media to shape public

[55] Sidney Milkis. *Theodore Roosevelt: Impact and Legacy*, Miller Center, University of Virginia, Web site: https://millercenter.org/president/theodoreroosevelt/impact-and-legacy, accessed June 2020.
[56] Thomas A Bailey. *Presidential Greatness: The Image and the Man from George Washington to the Present*, New York, New York: Appleton Century, 1966, p. 308.

opinion. He was the first President whose election was based more on the individual than the political party. When people voted Republican in 1904, they were generally casting their vote for Roosevelt the man instead of for him as the standard-bearer of the Republican Party. The most popular President up to his time, Roosevelt used his enthusiasm to win votes, to shape issues, and to mold opinions. In the process, he changed the executive office forever."[57]

The Political Legacy of Woodrow Wilson (1856 – 1924).

- "Like Jefferson, Wilson is easier to tab as a great man than as a great President. Both served long enough to see their early laurels wither during their last months in office. Until his collapse in September 1919, Wilson had rung up an amazing record as a leader. With unprecedented energy, he propelled through Congress an effective legislative program implementing his New Freedom – precursor of the New Deal. As a wartime evangel, Mr. Wilson led the nation on a holy crusade with spectacular success, considering his lack of military preparedness. A great leader (of the lone-wolf type), a great politician (the "regulars" were not too happy), a great phrase-maker, a great idealist, a great orator, a great preacher-moralist,

---

[57] Sidney Milkis. *Theodore Roosevelt: Impact and Legacy*, Miller Center, University of Virginia, Web site: https://millercenter.org/president/theodoreroosevelt/impact-and-legacy, accessed June 2020.

he was also a significant failure- at least in the short run. Instead of leading his people into the promised land, he led them into the fog and bog of disillusionment and frustration, where they fell under the spell of false prophets like Harding. His campaign to educate the masses on their new responsibilities had been too little and too late. The peace treaty which he co-authored, but which his people refused to accept on his terms, bred another war from whose ashes the United Nations rose. In this sense, Wilson, like Columbus, was a successful failure – a temporary failure but a success twenty-five years and millions of war dead later."[58]

- "As an influence on the nation and future politics, Wilson ranks behind only Washington, Lincoln, Franklin Roosevelt, and Jefferson in importance."[59]

- "Wilson's spectacular successes at home are substantially canceled out by his failures abroad, including his supreme failure as a peacemaker. He belongs with the Greats, where the experts

---

[58] Thomas A Bailey. *Presidential Greatness: The Image and the Man from George Washington to the Present*, New York, New York: Appleton Century, 1966, p. 311.

[59] *The Legacy of Woodrow Wilson*, The American Experience, Public Broadcasting Service, web site: https://www.pbs.org/wgbh/americanexperience/features/wilson-legacy/, accessed June 2020.

put him if we consider the first six years. He raises no higher than Near Great if that high when we consider all eight years, including the two when he was a shadow President broken on the wheel of fate."[60]

> **So can we most greatly help our beloved nation in time of need, our cause in common. I welcome your support. I honor myself in honoring you.**

An hour later, at 8:30 p.m., Governor Roosevelt's train sped eastward, carrying him to the White House and into history. Behind him, he left the most memorable day in the annals of McCook. He had singled out the old man who lived in the stucco house on upper Main street as "the very perfect, gentle knight of American progressive ideals."[61]

---

[60] Bailey. p. 312.

[61] Richard L. Neuberger and Stephen B. Kahn. *"Integrity: The Life of George W. Norris,"* New York, New York: The Vanguard Press, 1937, pp. 298 – 302.

V - The Ultimate Analysis of History

While Mr. Roosevelt departed McCook on that early autumn evening, his message hung in the midwestern air. As the crowd dispersed, the Governor's words dispersed in the fading sunlight as the campaign moved on to its "rendezvous with destiny."[1]

Nonetheless, his remarks laid out an enduring template for excellence in public service. This excerpt from his speech at McCook intertwines a concept of legacy with duty.

[1] Franklin Delano Roosevelt. *Renomination Speech for the Presidency*, The American Presidency Project, University of California, Santa Barbara, web site: https://www.presidency.ucsb.edu/documents/acceptance-speech-for-the-renomination-for-the-presidency-philadelphia-pa, accessed July 2020.

The Sunset At McCook

In our long national history we have seen in every decade the rise of *public servants to positions of great power and acclaim.*

In my studies of our history have always been deeply interested in the fact that *the appraisal of the greatness of statesmen by their contemporaries has often been completely reversed by a later verdict.*

If you will take even the history of any one State during a given *ten years* you will find a *de facto leadership and a temporary acclaim for many political leaders whose very names are wholly forgotten a generation later.*

We should remember that the *ultimate analysis of history* asks the answer to questions which are not concerned so much with what you and I, in these modern days, call ballyhoo, or headlines, as they are with much simpler fundamentals."

History asks:

"Did the man have *integrity?*"

"Did the man have *unselfishness?*"

"Did the man have *courage.*"

"Did the man have *consistency?*"

And if the individual under the *scrutiny of the historic microscope measured up to an affirmative answer to these questions then history has set him down as great indeed in the pages of all the years to come.*

A Passage from Franklin Delano Roosevelt's Speech
At Red Willow County Fairgrounds,
McCook, Nebraska on September 28, 1932
(Source: New York Times, September 29, 1932)

V – The Ultimate Analysis of History

The astute nature of his message lingers to this day and begs the resolution of several questions. Among them are, does it matter if public servants incorporate integrity, unselfishness, courage, and consistency in the fulfillment of their duties? What is their legacy if they build a career founded on these principles?

In a classic existentialist essay "The Tragic Sense of Life," Spanish philosopher Miguel de Unamuno reflects the public's compulsive concern with "legacy." He describes the "tremendous struggle to singularize ourselves, to survive in some way in the memory of others and posterity. It is this struggle that gives tone, color, and character to our society."[2]

Most political analysts adhere to the belief that being preoccupied with being remembered after leaving office is an inherent part of politics. To accomplish this, many politicians justify their decisions by a fixation on establishing a positive legacy. This impulse overrides a common creed that their only motive is reelection.

In 2017, several researchers from the Stanford University School of Business looked closely at the issue of political legacies.[3] They

---

[2] Christian Fong, Neil Malhotra and Yotam Margalit. *Political Legacies*, Palo Alto, California: 2017, p. 32.
[3] *Political Legacies*, Palo Alto, California: 2017.

found that the concept is viable. Citizens do remember politicians and debate their legacies after they have passed from active political life.

In a survey of 437 public officials serving at the federal level, they ascertained that about a third reported that being remembered matters a lot to them. They view legacy considerations as necessary even though they are pessimistic about the public's capacity to recognize their accomplishments.[4] This effort was a groundbreaking initiative to a phenomenon that guides much of the country's public policy administration.

They defined a political legacy as "either a concrete policy achievement or a memory, feeling, or idea that is associated with a politician and endures after they leave."[5] Their description highlights that there are two components of a political legacy, both hard and soft.

A hard political legacy centers on tangible changes and achievements, such as signing a treaty with a foreign government. A politician's hard legacy produces a stream of payoffs that starts when the

---

[4] *Political Legacies*, Palo Alto, California: 2017.
[5] *Political Legacies*, Palo Alto, California: 2017.

V - The Ultimate Analysis of History

policy is enacted and ends when replaced or repealed. Hard legacies can, therefore, be an elaboration on the "good policy" motivation.

Soft legacies relate to "collective memories," which are the aggregated individual memories of members of a group. They are a vision or a governing philosophy that influences future policy deliberations, as well as a set of shared experiences and memories that linger in the public mind. Soft legacies can also affect how future generations approach related but distinct policy challenges.

The concern with both hard and soft legacies can motivate actions while in office. Yet one's preoccupation with their quiet heritage may not necessarily be due to vanity or fame-seeking. There are strong instrumental reasons for a politician to invest in cultivating their soft legacy. For one, it may be that the durability of the politician's hard legacy is predicated on their quiet legacy generating a halo effect primarily in the specific domains associated with the politician's expertise or enduring achievements.

Despite their motivating influence, political figures are relatively pessimistic about the public's propensity to remember their contributions. About half believe that the public will not remember them within five years of their departure from office. Further, only 10% suppose they will be on the minds of the people for at least a decade.[6]

---

[6] *Political Legacies*, Palo Alto, California: 2017.

This dilemma does not deter them from not thinking about or acting to cement their legacies. Realizing that the mass public may forget them, they often refocus on impacting smaller geographic units.

Public Surveys note that only a small subset of politicians are capable of building enduring legacies. Most prominent are former United States presidents. The public remembers presidents at a very high rate, typically above 90% and decays very slowly since they left office.[7] Other offices do not fare as well as the presidents. The proportion of people who remember a president drops four percentage points in the 20 years after they leave the office. In contrast, the portion retaining a Speaker of the House drops 16 percentage points, and the proportion remembering a Secretary of State drops 32 percentage points over a similar time interval. The researchers did not examine the legacies of Members of Congress other than the Speaker of the House.

Having established that at least some politicians have strong legacies, we next turn to the question of whether or not the memories associated with these politicians are politically consequential. If people merely remembered that a particular individual held public office and nothing more, then legacies would be an uninteresting phenomenon. If people remembered biographical trivia and scandals, then memories of past politicians would mostly be irrelevant to current political events.

---

[7] *Political Legacies*, Palo Alto, California: 2017.

V – The Ultimate Analysis of History

The majority of memories are simple descriptions and personal characteristics which includes the office the politician held, the party of which the politician was a member, and biographic details Affective evaluations are also quite common (e.g., Jim Wright was "good," George H.W. Bush was "horrible"). More importantly, respondents are relatively likely to have memories of presidents that relate directly to public policy.

The combination of affective evaluations and policy-relevant memories suggests a vital role in political legacies. If a citizen remembers that a past politician whom he such as values supported a specific policy when debated, then that citizen is probably more likely to support that policy today. In that way, the politician's legacy influences contemporary debates.

The logical next step is determining what factors contribute to a political legacy. As we have seen, the most dominant inheritance is that of the chief executive, and this is where the strongest traits will surface. A noted Mexican academic researched this issue in 2014. While it focuses upon the Mexican Presidency, its relevance to United States political affairs is, for the most part, similar.

Positive and Negative Features of
(Mexican) Presidential Legacy[8]

Feature	Percentage
Ability to reform the existing institutions	33%
Authoritarianism	24%
Corruption	24%
Good economic performance	17%
Leadership/state vision	12%
Incapacity to govern	12%
Economic mismanagement	12%
Lack of leadership/ Lack of state vision	9%
Defense of national sovereignty	8%
Not bounded by institutions/breaks the law	8%
Follows the rules/limited by constraints	7%
Stabilized the country	6%
Honesty	5%
Capacity to conciliate among different groups	5%
Good diplomatic relations	4%
Submissive to foreign interests	4%
Efficacy/get things done	2%
Not working for the citizenry	2%
Inability to bargain	1.6%
Populism	1.2%
Nepotism	1.1%
Inability to reform	1%
Knowledge of society's problems	.7%
Bargaining abilities	.6%
Sincere concern for people's problems	.4%
Good working team/cabinet	.1%
Corrupt working team/cabinet	.1%

---

[8] Vidal Romero. *Of Love and Hate: Understanding the Determinants of Presidential Legacies*, Political Research Quarterly, Volume 67, Number 1, March 2014, p. 130.

V - The Ultimate Analysis of History

Franklin Roosevelt, in his remarks at McCook, remarked on personal qualities as a vital factor that contributes to a positive political legacy. Researchers do not often query the public on integrity, unselfishness, courage, and consistency. Their surveys indicate that honesty is not a major factor toward achieving a positive legacy.[9]

A study by Steven Greene on the American Presidency noted that "competence has a greater impact on how citizens view the president's performance than does integrity."[10]

One analysis of the topic states that a person evaluates the president, in part, as a person.[11] Character assessments provide hints about the elements of the president's performance to which individuals do not or cannot pay attention. Thus, by relying upon evaluations of the president's character, individuals can arrive at a comprehensive assessment without exerting the effort to monitor everything he says or does.

Aside from performance, the public, or at least part of it, wants the country's leader to be a person of integrity, a moral example, and a

---

[9] Romero. *Of Love and Hate: Understanding the Determinants of Presidential Legacies*, Political Research Quarterly, p. 130.

[10] Steven Green. *The Role of Character Assessments in Presidential Approval*, American Politics Research, Volume 29, Number 2, March 2001, p. 202.

[11] Brian Newman. *Integrity and Presidential Approval*, 1980 - 2000. The Public Opinion quarterly, Autumn 2003, Volume 67, Number 3, p. 339.

trustworthy authority.[12] A 1979 Gallup Poll found that 66 percent of respondents thought that "high ethical standards" were an essential presidential trait.[13]

To illustrate the relative significance of integrity on presidential legacy, the Siena College Research Institute Presidential Expert Poll of 2018 listed the ratings of United States presidents in order of leadership parameters. The following chart lists the top ten presidents in order of perceived integrity compared with their overall score.

Siena College Research Institute
Siena's Sixth Presidential Expert Poll
(1982 – 2018)[14]

President	Integrity	Overall Rank
George Washington	1	1
Abraham Lincoln	2	2
Jimmy Carter	3	26
John Adams	4	14
Dwight Eisenhower	5	6
James Madison	7	7
Theodore Roosevelt	8	4
Harry Truman	9	9
Gerald Ford	10	27

---

[12] Newman. *Integrity and Presidential Approval*, 1980 - 2000. p. 339.

[13] Brian Newman. *Integrity and Presidential Approval*, 1980 - 2000. The Public Opinion quarterly, Autumn 2003, Volume 67, Number 3, p. 340.

[14] *America's Presidents: Greatest and Worst*, Siena Research Institute, Siena College, Loudonville, New York, February 13, 2019.

V - The Ultimate Analysis of History

In essence, citizens expect their leaders to both be competent and hold an ethical standard superior to the people they serve.

Thomas Jefferson stated in 1796 the following maxim, which summarizes the issues associated with political legacies as they apply to the United States presidency.

"No man will ever bring out
Of the Presidency the reputation
Which carries him into it[15]

---

[15] Thomas Jefferson. *Thomas Jefferson Encyclopedia*, web site: https://www.monticello.org/site/research-and-collections/no-man-will-ever-bring-out-office-reputation-which-carries-him-it, accessed July 2020.

VI - The "Most Able" Senators
Serving in the 76th United States Congress -
A Case Study of Political Legacies

"The moment a person forms a theory,
His imagination sees in every object only the tracts which favor that theory.
But it is too early to form theories on those antiquities.
We must wait with patience until more facts are collected."[1]

Thomas Jefferson

In the previous chapter, we developed theories on the concept of political legacy from reviews of research analyses and the speech given by Franklin Roosevelt at McCook, Nebraska, on September 28, 1932.

As noted by Thomas Jefferson in 1787, we now present more facts to validate the hypotheses that integrity, unselfishness, courage, and consistency form the bedrock of a definite political legacy.

Since George W. Norris was the recipient of these accolades by Mr. Roosevelt, we focus upon his legacy as well as four other Senators named in 1939 as the ablest serving in the Upper House by a study conducted by Life magazine.

---

[1] Thomas Jefferson. *From Thomas Jefferson to Charles Thomson, 20 September 1787*, U.S. National Archives Founders Online, web site: https://founders.archives.gov/documents/Jefferson/01-12-02-0152#:~:text=The%20moment%20a%20person%20forms,till%20more%20facts%20are%20collected., accessed July 2020.

The Sunset At McCook

To set the stage, we must first understand the nature of the positions that these public servants held by a review of documents that form the bedrock of the United States Senate.

Overshadowing the issue is the statement by John Jay in the Federalist papers who spoke of United States Senators as "men of talents and integrity."[2]

---

[2] David S Broder. *What Makes A Great Senator*, New York, New York: New York Times, June 14, 1964, p. SM15.

VI – The "Most Able" Senators
Serving in the 76th United States Congress –
A Case Study of Political Legacies

"As the select assemblies for choosing the President, as well as the State legislatures who appoint the senators, will in general be composed of the most enlightened and respectable citizens, there is reason to presume that their attention and their votes will be directed to those men only who have become the *most distinguished by their abilities and virtue,* and in whom *the people perceive just grounds for confidence.*

The Constitution manifests very particular attention to this object.

By excluding men under thirty-five from the first office, and those under thirty from the second, it confines the electors to men of whom the people have had time to form a judgment, and with respect to whom *they will not be liable to be deceived by those brilliant appearances of genius and patriotism, which, like transient meteors, sometimes mislead as well as dazzle.*

If the observation be well founded, that wise kings will always be served by able ministers, it is fair to argue, that as an assembly of select electors possess, in a greater degree than kings, the means of extensive and accurate information relative to men and characters, so will their appointments bear at least equal marks of discretion and discernment.

The inference which naturally results from these considerations is this, that the President and senators so chosen will always be of the number of those who *best understand our national interests,* whether considered in relation to the several States or to foreign nations, who are *best able to promote those interests,* and *whose reputation for integrity inspires and merits confidence.*

With such men the power of making treaties may be safely lodged."

The Federalist Papers, Number 64, The Power of the Senate.[3]

---

[3] John Jay. *The Federalist Papers, Number 64,* web site: https://www.gutenberg.org/files/1404/1404-h/1404-h.htm#link2H_4_0064, accessed July 2020.

The Sunset At McCook

Then-Senator and future United States President John F. Kennedy elaborated on the difficulty of ascertaining greatness in the performance of Senators in 1957 while heading a committee to determine the five best of all time. He stated that there are no standard tests to apply to a Senator. Their talents may vary with his time and contributions limited by politics. In essence, to judge true greatness is nearly an impossible task.[4]

David Broder laid out in a 1964 New York Times article the tenets of "What Makes A Good Senator."[5] This distinguished journalist stated that popular generalizations of the ideal Senator often prove false to some degree. "One comes closer to the truth by noting that the best Senators, generally, are those who have acquired seniority and who use their powers, not simply for the advantage of their states, but also to serve their conception of the national interest."[6]

He notes that a combination of personal qualities and political circumstances marks the history of the best members. The first is the instinct that takes them to the heart of the issues of their time. They also must be diligent knowing the provisions of the bills they are debating than the majority of their colleagues. The third quality is the breadth of

---

[4] David S Broder. *What Makes A Great Senator*, New York, New York: New York Times, June 14, 1964, p. SM15.
[5] Ibid.
[6] Ibid.

VI - The "Most Able" Senators
Serving in the 76th United States Congress -
A Case Study of Political Legacies

interest by refusing to be bound by the local affairs of their state. The Pulitzer prize winner noted the public remembers the contributions of the public servant who can see beyond the borders of the body that elected them.

Broder went on to state that seniority, talent, diligence, breadth of vision, and a grasp of significant issues enables a Senator to contribute his full share to the making of national policy. His article went on to state that the Upper House has its shortcomings, but it is not arbitrary or capricious in the way it weighs its members and judges them for what they are. In time, undoubtedly, the Senate passes *fair judgment* on those who join its ranks.

FDR's McCook speech, the Federalist Papers, and David Broder's article on what makes a great Senator form the basis for our analysis of the political legacies of a selected group of George Norris' Depression-era associates in the U.S. Congress Upper House.

Since the 1930s and the speech at McCook, there have been numerous attempts to determine the relative competence of public servants at the federal level with widely varying degrees of success. When viewed from the context of the McCook speech is the fact that researchers don't include questions regarding integrity, unselfishness, courage, and consistency in their surveys. The generic terms "Character" or "Integrity" are often used in queries testifying to the effectiveness of political leaders. However, that is the limit of the inquiring on that subject. The common assumption is that proper ethics are needed to be effective in public administration and constitute the foundation of a superb reputation. However, they are not part of the quantifiable attributes of public service.

This limitation, notwithstanding a study of these surveys and reports, provides ancillary evidence of the viability of Franklin Roosevelt's thesis. In the sections that follow, an analysis of one of the most conspicuous studies of United States elected officials conducted in the Depression-era illustrates the relative integrity of FDR's hypothesis.

Future President John F. Kennedy explained the difficulty in judging the quality of a Senator in 1957. He stated that there are no standard tests to apply to a Senator. Their talents may vary with their era in office and, subsequently, contributions limited by politics. To judge his true greatness is nearly an impossible task."[7]

The article goes on to explain that popular generalizations of the ideal Senator often prove false, to some degree. "One comes closer to the truth by noting that the best Senators, generally, are those who have

---

[7] David S Broder. *What Makes A Great Senator*, New York, New York: New York Times, June 14, 1964, p. SM15.

VI - The "Most Able" Senators
Serving in the 76ᵗʰ United States Congress -
A Case Study of Political Legacies

acquired seniority and who use their powers, not simply for the advantage of their states, but also to serve their conception of the national interest."[8]

On March 20, 1939, Life Magazine, a popular periodical of the time, published the results of a survey to select the ablest Congressmen serving in the 76ᵗʰ United States Congress.[9] Earlier that month, on March 4, the Congress assembled in joint session to commemorate the 150ᵗʰ Anniversary of the first Congressional meeting. In recognition of the event, Life staff wrote to a highly selective group of 53 Washington correspondents who covered the Congress. The magazine's editors asked for their thoughts on which of the 531 Senators and Members of the House of Representatives inspired the highest respect and confidence.

In a confidential unsigned ballot each correspondent was asked to list those who they considered the ten ablest members of each House of Congress and to give each one a numerical rating on each of the following attributes:

---

[8] David S Broder. *What Makes A Great Senator*, New York, New York: New York Times, June 14, 1964, p. SM15.

[9] *Washington Correspondents Name Ablest Members of Congress In Life Poll*, Chicago, Illinois: Life Magazine, Volume 6, Number 12, March 20, 1939, pp. 13 - 17.

- *Integrity.* Does the elected official have principles and stick to them regardless of political expediency?
- *Intelligence.* Does the incumbent have a good head, and a sound stock of information, historical and current, to use it on?
- *Industry.* Does the Senator or Representative give his conscientious best to his job?
- *Influence.* Does the public servant have the political savvy and the personal charm and tact, to put his ideas and get things done?

The following section lists the top five incumbents from the United States Senate in the composite judgment of the 53 voting correspondents selected from leading news publications that covered the Congress at that time. The charts illustrate information gathered in the Life Magazine poll published in March 1939.

- Each correspondent ranked the elected official from 1 to 10. The numbers are the average of the "grade," which the voter awarded each candidate in Integrity, Intelligence, Industry, and Influence.
- "★" indicates composite top grade in each category.
- Final ranking was determined by point score, with each first-place vote-counting 10, each second-place 9, each third-place

eight down to 1 for tenth place. Thus, Senator Norris with 40 votes outranks Senator Borah with 46 because Norris topped the list of 20 voters while only 11 ranked Borah the Number 1 Senator.

The Sunset At McCook

GEORGE WILLIAM NORRIS
(1861 - 1944)

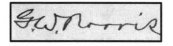

Political Offices[10]

MEMBER, UNITED STATES HOUSE OF REPRESENTATIVES
(1903 -1913)

UNITED STATES SENATOR (NEBRASKA)
(1913 - 1943)

Selected Vitae.[11]

- He was born in Sandusky County, Ohio, the son of a farmer.

- Worked as a school teacher, lawyer, and judge before entering Congress.

- Graduated from Northern Indiana Normal School and law school at Valparaiso University. The bar admitted him in 1883.

- In 1899 he married Pluma Lashley. The couple had three daughters. After she died in 1901, Norris married Ella Leonard. They had no children.

---

[10] *George W. Norris.* Wikipedia, web site: https://en.wikipedia.org/wiki/George_W._Norris, accessed July 2020.
[11] Wayne S. Cole. *Norris, George William,* American National Biography, web site: https://doi.org/10.1093/anb/9780198606697.article.0600476, published online February 2000, accessed July 2020.

VI - The "Most Able" Senators
Serving in the 76th United States Congress -
A Case Study of Political Legacies

- In 1892 he won election as county prosecuting attorney and, in 1895, judge of the Fourteenth Judicial District.

- Won a congressional seat in 1902 where he served five terms until 1913.

- Elected to the United States Senate in 1912 and served for thirty years (1913 - 1943).

- Defeated in 1942, he died at McCook, Nebraska, in 1944.

- Legislative Specialty: Public electric-power.[12]

General Comments on Legislative Record

- "A grand old man."[13]

- "Greatest liberal of them all."[14]

- "Has probably accomplished more than any other man in the Senate."[15]

- "Has slowed up in late years."[16]

---

[12] *Washington Correspondents Name Ablest Members of Congress In Life Poll*, Life Magazine, p. 16.

[13] *Washington Correspondents Name Ablest Members of Congress In Life Poll*, Life Magazine, p. 16.

[14] *Washington Correspondents Name Ablest Members of Congress In Life Poll*, Life Magazine, p. 16.

[15] *Washington Correspondents Name Ablest Members of Congress In Life Poll*, Life Magazine, p. 16.

[16] *Washington Correspondents Name Ablest Members of Congress In Life Poll*, Life Magazine, p. 16.

- "Fast-aging man now leaning on past achievements."[17]

- "Very perfect, gentle knight of American progressive ideals."[18]

- "Served his country and its people well through a long and honorable public career."[19]

Life Magazine Ablest Members of Congress 1939 Poll
Numeric Ratings
For Senator George W. Norris[20]

INTEGRITY	INTELLIGENCE	INDUSTRY	INFLUENCE	AVERAGE	VOTES	POINTS	PERSONALITY
96.9	85.1	81.5	83.8	86.8	40	297.5	"Quiet"
						Highest score in Senate	"Companionable"
							"Homebody"

---

[17] *Pat of the Senate*, New York Times, July 9, 1922.
[18] *George W. Norris.* Wikipedia.
[19] Wayne S. Cole. *Norris, George William,* American National Biography.
[20] *Washington Correspondents Name Ablest Members of Congress In Life Poll* , Life Magazine, p. 14.

VI - The "Most Able" Senators
Serving in the 76th United States Congress -
A Case Study of Political Legacies

Franklin Delano Roosevelt
Political Legacy Attributes
For Senator George W. Norris

Trait	Legacy
INTEGRITY	"Vast prestige and absolute integrity."[21] "Thinks he is the world's, only honest man."[22]
UNSELFISHNESS	"Neither presidents nor party organizations controlled his positions on public issues."[23]
COURAGE	"Respected in and out of Congress for his political courage."[24]

[21] *Washington Correspondents Name Ablest Members of Congress In Life Poll*, Life Magazine, p. 16.

[22] *Washington Correspondents Name Ablest Members of Congress In Life Poll*, Life Magazine, p. 16.

[23] Wayne S. Cole. *Norris, George William,* American National Biography.

[24] Wayne S. Cole. *Norris, George William,* American National Biography.

The Sunset At McCook

TRAIT	LEGACY
CONSISTENCY	"Probably accomplished more than any other in the Senate."[25] "Prided himself on his independence."[26]

[25] *Washington Correspondents Name Ablest Members of Congress In Life Poll*, Life Magazine, p. 16.

[26] Wayne S. Cole. *Norris, George William,* American National Biography.

VI - The "Most Able" Senators
Serving in the 76th United States Congress -
A Case Study of Political Legacies

WILLIAM EDGAR BORAH
(1865–1940)

Political Offices[27]

UNITED STATES SENATOR (IDAHO)
(1907 - 1940)

DEAN OF THE UNITED STATES SENATE
(1933 – 1940)

Selected Vitae

- He was born in Wayne County, Illinois, the son of a farmer.[28]

- He never finished high school.[29]

- Read law and passed the bar examination in 1887.[30]

- Legislative Specialties: Foreign Affairs, American Isolation.[31]

---

[27] William Borah, Wikipedia, web site:
https://en.wikipedia.org/wiki/William_Borah, accessed July 2020.
[28] Robert James Maddox. *Borah, William Edgar*, American National
Biography, web site:
https://doi.org/10.1093/anb/9780198606697.article.0600056, published
online February 2000, accessed July 2020.
[29] Maddox, *Borah*, American National Biography.
[30] Maddox, *Borah*, American National Biography.
[31] *Washington Correspondents Name Ablest Members of Congress In Life
Poll*, Chicago, Illinois: Life Magazine, Volume 6, Number 12, March 20,
1939, p. 16.

- She died in office.[32]

General Comments on Legislative Record

- "Aging, but still can deliver."[33]

- "His greatest contribution to statesmanship is stopping bad legislation."[34]

- "Best mind in the Senate."[35]

- "Starts more than he finishes."[36]

- "He gives up good ideas too soon."[37]

- "Now old and lazy."[38]

- "Useless in committee where constructive legislation is formulated."[39]

---

[32] *William Borah*, Wikipedia.
[33] *Washington Correspondents Name Ablest Members of Congress In Life Poll*, Life Magazine, p. 16.
[34] *Washington Correspondents Name Ablest Members of Congress In Life Poll*, Life Magazine, p. 16.
[35] *Washington Correspondents Name Ablest Members of Congress In Life Poll*, Life Magazine, p. 16.
[36] *Washington Correspondents Name Ablest Members of Congress In Life Poll*, Life Magazine, p. 16.
[37] *Washington Correspondents Name Ablest Members of Congress In Life Poll*, Life Magazine, p. 16.
[38] *Washington Correspondents Name Ablest Members of Congress In Life Poll*, Life Magazine, p. 16.
[39] *Washington Correspondents Name Ablest Members of Congress In Life Poll*, Life Magazine, p. 16.

VI – The "Most Able" Senators
Serving in the 76th United States Congress –
A Case Study of Political Legacies

- "Although he was more honorable, dedicated, and talented than most men who have sat in the Capitol's upper chamber, Borah was not a great senator."[40]

- "In 1936 Walter Lippmann neatly characterized Borah's political beliefs when he called the Senator an individualist who opposes all concentration of power, who is against private privilege and private monopoly, against political bureaucracy and centralized government."[41]

Life Magazine Ablest Members of Congress 1939 Poll
Numeric Ratings[42]
For Senator William E. Borah

INTEGRITY	INTELLIGENCE	INDUSTRY	INFLUENCE	AVERAGE	VOTES	POINTS	PERSONALITY
88.4	95.6	75.2	80.4	84.9	46	287	"Friendly"
	Best Rating in Senate					Second Highest Rating in Senate	"Dignified" "Homebody"

---

[40] John Milton Cooper, Jr. *William E. Borah, Political Thespian*, The Pacific Northwest Quarterly, October 1965, Volume 56, Number 4, pp. 145 – 153.

[41] Cooper. *William E. Borah, Political Thespian*, p. 148.

[42] *Washington Correspondents Name Ablest Members of Congress In Life Poll* , Life Magazine, p. 14.

The Sunset At McCook

Franklin Delano Roosevelt
Political Legacy Attributes
For Senator William E. Borah

TRAIT	LEGACY
INTEGRITY	"Vast prestige and absolute integrity."[43] "A "moral force" in the halls of Congress."[44] "Valued by friend or foe on account of his courage, honesty, and decent method of fighting."[45]

---

[43] Maddox. *Borah*, American National Biography.

[44] Miller. *The West: The Lion of Idaho"....William E. Borah, More Than a "Little American*, History News Network.

[45] *William Borah*, Wikipedia.

VI - The "Most Able" Senators
Serving in the 76th United States Congress -
A Case Study of Political Legacies

TRAIT	LEGACY
UNSELFISHNESS	"His willingness to speak out on controversial issues and his indifference to party loyalty earned him a national following."[46] "Always something of a maverick, he voted his conscience, often against the party line."[47] "His strength with the people...his simplicity, his approachability, his kindliness, his human sympathy. It was genuine, and the people felt it. Borah was their friend."[48]

---

[46] Maddox. *Borah*, American National Biography.

[47] Miller. *The West: The Lion of Idaho"....William E. Borah, More Than a "Little American,* History News Network.

[48] Claudius O. Johnson, *William E. Borah, The People's Choice*, The Pacific Northwest Quarterly, January 1953, Volume 44, Number 1 , pp. 15 - 22.

The Sunset At McCook

TRAIT	LEGACY
COURAGE	"Utterly fearless, no matter how unpopular the cause."[49] "Almost as suspicious of U.S. presidents as he was of foreign nations, Borah perceived threats everywhere."[50] "A stout defender of civil liberties."[51]
CONSISTENCY	"The most effective and virile leader in the Senate."[52] "The topflight orator of the Senate."[53] "A reputation for futility."[54]

[49] Miller. *The West: The Lion of Idaho".... William E. Borah, More Than a "Little American*, History News Network.

[50] *William Borah*, Wikipedia.

[51] Maddox. *Borah, William Edgar*, American National Biography.

[52] Miller. *The West: The Lion of Idaho".... William E. Borah, More Than a "Little American*, History News Network.

[53] *Washington Correspondents Name Ablest Members of Congress In Life Poll*, Life Magazine, p. 14.

[54] Miller. *The West: The Lion of Idaho".... William E. Borah, More Than a "Little American*, History News Network.

VI – The "Most Able" Senators Serving in the 76th United States Congress – A Case Study of Political Legacies

ROBERT FERDINAND WAGNER
(1877 - 1953)

Political Offices[55]

NEW YORK STATE ASSEMBLY
(1905 - 1908)

NEW YORK STATE SENATE
(1909 - 1918)

UNITED STATES SENATOR (NEW YORK)
(1927 - 1949)

Selected Vitae

- Born in Prussia and migrated with his family to the United States in 1886.[56]

- Worked through City College of New York from which he graduated in 1898.

---

[55] Robert F. Wagner, Wikipedia. web site:
https://en.wikipedia.org/wiki/Robert_F._Wagner, accessed July 2020.
[56] Paula Eldot. *Wagner, Robert F.,* American National Biography, web site:
https://doi.org/10.1093/anb/9780198606697.article.0600678, published online February 2000, accessed July 2020.

- He held assorted jobs such as newsboy, grocery boy, and political worker.

- Wagner graduated from New York Law School in 1898 and gained admission to the bar in 1900.[57]

- Married in 1908 to Margaret Marie McTague and widowed in 1919. He raised their only child, Robert Ferdinand Wagner, Jr., who ultimately became mayor of New York City.[58]

- Legislative Specialties: Social Legislation.[59]

- Senator Robert F. Wagner died in 1953.[60]

General Comments on Legislative Record

- "Sincere, social-minded humanitarian."[61]

- "Most useful Senator in a constructive way."[62]

- "His influence is great because of Administration backing."[63]

---

[57] Eldot. *Wagner, Robert F.,* American National Biography.

[58] Eldot. *Wagner, Robert F.,* American National Biography.

[59] *Washington Correspondents Name Ablest Members of Congress In Life Poll*, Chicago, Illinois: Life Magazine, Volume 6, Number 12, March 20, 1939, p. 16.

[60] *Robert F. Wagner,* Wikipedia, web site: https://en.wikipedia.org/wiki/Robert_F._Wagner, accessed July 2020.

[61] *Washington Correspondents Name Ablest Members of Congress In Life Poll* , Life Magazine, p. 16.

[62] *Washington Correspondents Name Ablest Members of Congress In Life Poll* , Life Magazine, p. 16.

[63] *Washington Correspondents Name Ablest Members of Congress In Life Poll* , Life Magazine, p. 16.

VI - The "Most Able" Senators Serving in the 76ᵗʰ United States Congress - A Case Study of Political Legacies

- "His laws would be better if he did not play Labor politics."[64]

- "Respected for his political acumen within his state."[65]

- "Most important legislative achievements include the National Industrial Recovery Act (1933) and the Wagner-Steagall Housing Act (1937)."[66]

Life Magazine Ablest Members of Congress 1939 Poll Numeric Ratings[67] For Senator Robert Ferdinand Wagner

INTEGRITY	INTELLIGENCE	INDUSTRY	INFLUENCE	AVERAGE	VOTES	POINTS	PERSONALITY
90.0	84.5	88.9	80.4	86	40	261.5 Third highest score in Senate	"Simple" "Genial" "Slow-Moving"

---

[64] *Washington Correspondents Name Ablest Members of Congress In Life Poll*, Life Magazine, p. 16.

[65] Thomas E. Hachey. *American Profiles on Capitol Hill: A Confidential Study for the British Foreign Office in 1943*, The Wisconsin Magazine of History, Volume 57, Number 2, Winter 1973 - 1974, pp. 147.

[66] *Robert F. Wagner*, Wikipedia.

[67] *Washington Correspondents Name Ablest Members of Congress In Life Poll*, Life Magazine, p. 14.

The Sunset At McCook

Franklin Delano Roosevelt
Political Legacy Attributes
For Senator Robert F. Wagner

Trait	Legacy
INTEGRITY	"His vision of justice extended to all races and classes in the American community."[68] "Inability and character, in honesty of purpose and manliness of action, Senator Wagner has been an inspiration to younger legislators and a beacon light to men older than him in years. He was the friend of the laboring man and the defender of women and children who have to earn their bread by the sweat of their brow and yet he never was a demagogue. All the gold in the world could not buy him; all the beckonings of ambition could not induce him to abandon the righteous cause and the issue that was true. He has served the people well."[69]

---

[68] Eldot. *Wagner, Robert F.,* American National Biography.
[69] *Robert F. Wagner,* Spartacus Educational, web site: https://spartacus-educational.com/USARwagner.htm, accessed July 2020.

VI – The "Most Able" Senators
Serving in the 76ᵗʰ United States Congress –
A Case Study of Political Legacies

TRAIT	LEGACY
UNSELFISHNESS	"Wagner's rise from modest circumstances left a deep imprint on his character…He established himself as a tireless spokesman for the lower and working classes."[70]
COURAGE	"Alerted early to the menace of Nazism, Wagner pressed for admission of Jewish refugees to Palestine and later for the Jewish nation there."[71]

---

[70]Roger Biles. *Robert F. Wagner, Franklin D. Roosevelt, and Social Welfare Legislation in the New Deal*, Presidential Studies Quarterly, Winter 1998, Volume 28, Number 1, p. 140.

[71] Eldot. *Wagner, Robert F.*, American National Biography.

The Sunset At McCook

TRAIT	LEGACY
CONSISTENCY	"Tenacity 1,000%"[72] "With average abilities and almost no personal following, he gets results by plugging."[73] "A typical anti-Nazi German Democrat who has supported all the administration measures, being usually well in advance of them."[74]

---

[72] *Washington Correspondents Name Ablest Members of Congress In Life Poll*, Life Magazine, p. 16.

[73] *Washington Correspondents Name Ablest Members of Congress In Life Poll*, Life Magazine, p. 16.

[74] Thomas E. Hachey. *American Profiles on Capitol Hill: A Confidential Study for the British Foreign Office in 1943*, The Wisconsin Magazine of History, Volume 57, Number 2, Winter 1973 - 1974, p. 147.

VI – The "Most Able" Senators
Serving in the 76th United States Congress –
A Case Study of Political Legacies

JAMES FRANCIS BYRNES
(1882 - 1972)

Political Offices[75]

MEMBER, UNITED STATES HOUSE OF REPRESENTATIVES
(1911 - 1925)

UNITED STATES SENATOR (SOUTH CAROLINA)
(1931 - 1941)

ASSOCIATE JUSTICE OF THE SUPREME COURT OF THE UNITED STATES
(1941 - 1942)

UNITED STATES SECRETARY OF STATE
(1945 - 1947)

GOVERNOR OF SOUTH CAROLINA
(1951 - 1955)

Selected Vitae

- Born and raised in Charleston, South Carolina, the son of a city clerk and dressmaker.[76]

---

[75] *James F. Byrnes*, Wikipedia. web site:
https://en.wikipedia.org/wiki/James_F._Byrnes, accessed July 2020.
[76] David L. Anderson. *Byrnes, James Francis,* American National Biography, web site: https://doi.org/10.1093/anb/9780198606697.article.0700043, published online February 2000, accessed July 2020.

- His father died before Byrnes was born. At age fourteen, he left school to help support his family. To obtain a position as a court stenographer, he misrepresented his year of birth as 1879, which he used for the rest of his life.

- Under the tutelage of two judges, he was schooled and read law. He passed the South Carolina bar exam in 1903.

- Byrnes married Maude Busch in 1906. The couple had no children.

- One of the very few politicians to serve in all three branches of the American federal government while also being active in state government.[77]

- "Byrnes was one of the most powerful politicians in the United States in the 1930s and 1940s."[78]

- Selected as "Man of the Year" by Time Magazine for 1946.[79]

- Legislative Specialties: Relief Reform, Government Reorganization, Economy.[80]

- James F. Byrnes died in 1972 at his home in Columbia, South Carolina.[81]

---

[77] *James F. Byrnes*, Wikipedia. web site: https://en.wikipedia.org/wiki/James_F._Byrnes, accessed July 2020.

[78] Anderson. *Byrnes, James Francis,* American National Biography.

[79] *The Nations: The Year of the Bullbat,* Time Magazine, New York, New York, January 6, 1947.

[80] *Washington Correspondents Name Ablest Members of Congress In Life Poll,* Life Magazine, p. 16.

[81] *James F. Byrnes*, Wikipedia.

VI – The "Most Able" Senators
Serving in the 76th United States Congress –
A Case Study of Political Legacies

- Despite his multifaceted and significant career, Byrnes, except for his tenure as Secretary of State, has been largely ignored by scholars.[82]

General Comments on Legislative Record

- "A politician first."[83]

- "Too politically minded."[84]

Life Magazine Ablest Members of Congress 1939 Poll
Numeric Ratings[85]
For Senator James F. Byrnes

INTEGRITY	INTELLIGENCE	INDUSTRY	INFLUENCE	AVERAGE	VOTES	POINTS	PERSONALITY
81.6	87.0	87.1	87.7	85.8	40	257.5	"Simple"
						Fourth best score in Senate	"Suave" "Dapper"

Franklin Delano Roosevelt
Political Legacy Attributes
For Senator James F. Byrnes

---

[82] James L. Gormly, *Secretary of State James F. Byrnes, an Initial British Evaluation*, The South Carolina Historical Magazine, July 1978, p. 199.

[83] *Washington Correspondents Name Ablest Members of Congress In Life Poll*, Life Magazine, p. 16.

[84] *Washington Correspondents Name Ablest Members of Congress In Life Poll*, Life Magazine, p. 16.

[85] *Washington Correspondents Name Ablest Members of Congress In Life Poll*, Life Magazine, p. 14.

TRAIT	LEGACY
INTEGRITY	"Not overly strong on principle."[86] "For more than five decades, he remained a remarkable political strategist and dedicated public official."[87] "A good measure of personal integrity and political conscience have left him a poor man at the end of a highly successful public career."[88]
UNSELFISHNESS	"An able conciliator."[89] "A remarkable legislative strategist and unselfish wartime servant."[90]

[86] *Washington Correspondents Name Ablest Members of Congress In Life Poll*, Life Magazine, p. 14.
[87] Anderson. *Byrnes, James Francis,* American National Biography.
[88] Gormly, *Secretary of State James F. Byrnes, an Initial British Evaluation,* The South Carolina Historical Magazine, p. 200.
[89] *Washington Correspondents Name Ablest Members of Congress In Life Poll*, Life Magazine, p. 16.
[90] *James F. Byrnes*, New, York, New York: New York Times, April 10, 1972, p. 34.

VI - The "Most Able" Senators
Serving in the 76th United States Congress -
A Case Study of Political Legacies

TRAIT	LEGACY
COURAGE	"He seems in sum to be a man of accommodating temper, imbued with a genuine desire to serve his country and to work for a better world, but not of strong character, settled convictions, or a capacity to fight too hard for them against strong odds."[91]

"The undeniable justice of desegregation overrode his notion of what was practical in the South."[92]

"Byrnes would not be noted for his courage in leading his fellow southerners in a new direction for closer relations between races."[93]

"It was sad, then, that he should have ended his active political career as a kind of reconstructed – or reconverted – Governor of South Carolina, in full revolt against the liberalism he had once done much to advance, trying to hold the line for segregation and reaction."[94] |

[91] James L. Gormly, *Secretary of State James F. Byrnes, an Initial British Evaluation*, The South Carolina Historical Magazine, July 1978, p. 201.

TRAIT	LEGACY
CONSISTENCY	"The Senate's hardest worker."[95] "Best legislator on Capitol Hill."[96] "Tops as a conniver."[97]

---

[92]. David L. Anderson. *Byrnes, James Francis,* American National Biography, web site: https://doi.org/10.1093/anb/9780198606697.article.0700043, published online February 2000, accessed July 2020.

[93] Thomas S. Morgan. *James F. Byrnes and the Politics of Segregation,* The Historian, Summer 1994, Volume 56, Number 4, p. 651.

[94] *James F. Byrnes,* New, York, New York: New York Times, April 10, 1972, p. 34.

[95] *Washington Correspondents Name Ablest Members of Congress In Life Poll*, Life Magazine, p. 16.

[96] *Washington Correspondents Name Ablest Members of Congress In Life Poll*, Life Magazine, p. 16.

[97] *Washington Correspondents Name Ablest Members of Congress In Life Poll*, Life Magazine, p. 16.

VI – The "Most Able" Senators
Serving in the 76th United States Congress –
A Case Study of Political Legacies

BYRON PATTON "PAT" HARRISON
(1881 - 1941)

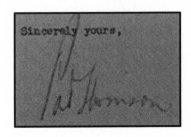

Political Offices[98]

MEMBER, UNITED STATES HOUSE OF REPRESENTATIVES
(1911 -1919)

UNITED STATES SENATOR (MISSISSIPPI)
(1919 - 1941)

PRESIDENT PRO TEMPORE OF THE UNITED STATES SENATE
(1941)

Selected Vitae

- Born in Crystal Springs, Mississippi, the son of a merchant.[99]

---

[98] *Pat Harrison*, Wikipedia, web site:
https://en.wikipedia.org/wiki/Pat_Harrison, accessed July 2020.
[99] Martha H. Swain. *Harrison, Pat,* American National Biography, web site:
https://doi.org/10.1093/anb/9780198606697.article.0600257, published
online February 2000, accessed July 2020.

- Worked as a newsboy and semi-pro baseball player.[100]

- After two years at what is now Louisiana State University (1899 – 1891), Harrison became a public school teacher while studying law at night. He began his legal practice in 1902.

- In 1905 he married Mary Edwina McInnis with whom he had five children. Three survived to adulthood.

- Harrison entered politics in 1906, serving for two terms as a district attorney in his state.

- Won a congressional seat in 1910 where he served four terms (1911 – 1919).

- Elected to the United States Senate in 1919 and served until he died in 1941.

- Died in Washington, D.C., six months after being named president pro tempore of the Senate.

- Legislative Specialties: Taxes, Economy.[101]

General Comments on Legislative Record

- "He is of the Virginia Harrisons, from the same strain as William Henry Harrison and Benjamin Harrison, Presidents of the United States."[102]

---

[100] *Washington Correspondents Name Ablest Members of Congress In Life Poll*, Life Magazine, p. 16.
[101] *Washington Correspondents Name Ablest Members of Congress In Life Poll*, Life Magazine, p. 16.
[102] *Pat of the Senate*, New York, New York, New York Times, July 9, 1922, Section S, p. 83.

VI – The "Most Able" Senators
Serving in the 76th United States Congress –
A Case Study of Political Legacies

- "He elevated horse-trading to statecraft."[103]

- "The best wangler in the Senate."[104]

- "Conservative balance wheel."[105]

- "Best posted man on current events of any member of the Senate."[106]

- "Never the author of any major legislation, Harrison was the broker for the ideas of others. Through artful compromise and "horse-trading," Harrison was a master in the conference committee, where he could cajole opponents into retreating from unachievable demands."[107]

- "Harrison was a highly effective politician and a brilliant orator."[108]

- "Pat Harrison has been largely forgotten in the years since his death."[109]

---

[103] *Washington Correspondents Name Ablest Members of Congress In Life Poll*, Life Magazine, p. 16.

[104] *Washington Correspondents Name Ablest Members of Congress In Life Poll*, Life Magazine, p. 16.

[105] *Washington Correspondents Name Ablest Members of Congress In Life Poll*, Life Magazine, p. 16.

[106] *Pat of the Senate*, New York Times, July 9, 1922.

[107] Swain. *Harrison, Pat,* American National Biography.

[108] *Pat Harrison*, Wikipedia. web site: https://en.wikipedia.org/wiki/Pat_Harrison, accessed July 2020.

[109] Martha H. Swain. *Senator Pat Harrison: New Deal Wheel horse (1933 – 1941) Suspicious of His Load,* web site: www.mshistorynow.mdah.ms.gov?articles/374/senator-pat-harrison-new-deal-wheelhorse-suspicious-of-his-load-1933-1941, accessed July 2020.

Life Magazine Ablest Members of Congress 1939 Poll
Numeric Ratings
For Senator Pat Harrison[110]

INTEGRITY	INTELLIGENCE	INDUSTRY	INFLUENCE	AVERAGE	VOTES	POINTS	PERSONALITY
78.0	82.7	70.9	89.8	80.4	42	215.0	"Mellow"
			Highest score in Senate			Fifth best score in Senate	"Witty"

---

[110] *Washington Correspondents Name Ablest Members of Congress In Life Poll*, Life Magazine, p. 14.

VI - The "Most Able" Senators
Serving in the 76th United States Congress -
A Case Study of Political Legacies

Franklin Delano Roosevelt
Political Legacy Attributes
For Senator Pat Harrison

TRAIT	LEGACY
INTEGRITY	"The cunning fox of the Senate."[111] "A natural leader."[112] "Shrewd, smart as the devil."[113] "A Republican adversary once characterized him as "square, approachable, and intensely human"; he was never known to renege on a pledge."[114]

---

[111] *Washington Correspondents Name Ablest Members of Congress In Life Poll*, Life Magazine, p. 16.
[112] *Washington Correspondents Name Ablest Members of Congress In Life Poll*, Life Magazine, p. 16.
[113] *Washington Correspondents Name Ablest Members of Congress In Life Poll*, Life Magazine, p. 16.
[114] Swain. *Harrison, Pat,* American National Biography.

The Sunset At McCook

TRAIT	LEGACY
UNSELFISHNESS	"Harrison's liberalism, like many of his southern colleagues, was pragmatic and fell far short of embracing any social reforms that would threaten prevailing race relations in the South."[115]
COURAGE	"Harrison Rebuffs Klan."[116]
CONSISTENCY	"Downright lazy."[117] "Not very industrious."[118] "Harrison gained a reputation as an effective gadfly."[119]

---

[115] Swain. *Harrison, Pat,* American National Biography.

[116] *Harrison Rebuffs Klan*, New York, New York, New York times, August 27, 1927, p. 14.

[117] *Washington Correspondents Name Ablest Members of Congress In Life Poll*, Life Magazine, p. 16.

[118] *Washington Correspondents Name Ablest Members of Congress In Life Poll*, Life Magazine, p. 16.

[119] Swain. *Harrison, Pat,* American National Biography.

VI – The "Most Able" Senators
Serving in the 76th United States Congress –
A Case Study of Political Legacies

The 116th United States Congress is currently in session, allowing several generations to distill the legacies of the senators named as most able in 1939. The feasibility of the Roosevelt theory that a positive political legacy is based on substantive accomplishment and exemplary personal qualities remains as accurate today as it was in during the Sunset at McCook in 1932.

"Reputation is an idle and most false imposition,
oft got without merit and lost without deserving.
You have lost no reputation at all
unless you repute yourself such a loser."

William Shakespeare
No Fear, Act 2 Scene 3
Othello, 1604

Bibliography

Ambar, S. (n.d.). *Woodrow Wilson: Impact and Legacy*. Retrieved June 2020, from https://www.millercenter.org/president/wilson/impact-and-legacy

Anderson, D. L. (2000, February). *Byrnes, James Francis*. Retrieved from American National Biography: https://doi.org/10.1093/anb/9780198606697.article.0700043

Bailey, T. A. (1966). *Presidential Greatness: The Image and the Man from George Washington to the Present.* New York: Van Rees Press.

Barber, J. D. (2009). *The Presidential Character: Predicting Performance in the White House (Fourth Edition).* New York: Routledge.

Biles, R. (Winter 1998). Robert F. Wagner, Franklin D. Roosevelt, and Social Welfare Legislation in the New Deal. *Presidential Studies Quarterly, Volume 28, Number 1*, 139 - 152.

Blessing, T. H. (December 1983). The Presidential Performance Study: A Progress Report. *Journal of American History, Volume 70, No. 3*, 535 - 555.

Blessing, T. H. (Summer 1995). Three Swings and Ten Dynasties: The Temporal-Historical Aspects of Presidential Performance. *Presidential Studies Quarterly, Volume 25, No. 3*, 457 - 477.

Boettinger, J. (1932, September 29). Roosevelt and Norris Swap Trade Lasts. *Chicago Tribune*, p. 1.

Brian F. Crisp, K. K. (2004). Teh Reputations Legislators Build: With Whom Should Representatives Collaborate? *The American Political Science Review Volume 98, Number 4*, 703 - 716.

Brian F. Schaffner, W. J. (2003, May). Tactical and Contextual Determinants of U.S. Senators' Approval Ratings. *Legislative Studies Quarterly, Volume 28, Number 2*, pp. 203 - 223.

Brinkley, A. (2000, February). *Roosevelt, Franklin Delano*. Retrieved June 20, 2020, from American National Biography: https://www.anb.org/view/10.1093/anb/9780198606697.001.0001/anb-9780198606697-e-0600567

Broder, D. S. (1964, June 14). What Makes A Great Senator. *The New York Times*, pp. pp. 270, 332, 333.

Burlingame, M. (n.d.). *Abraham Lincoln: Impact and Legacy*. Retrieved June 2020, from https://millercenter.org/president/lincoln/impact-and-legacy

Bibliography

Calabresi, S. G. (2000, November Nov. 16, 2000). *Ranking the Presidents.*
    Retrieved June 19, 2020, from Wall Street Journal:
    https://www.wsj.com/articles/SB974336784441980753

Canham, E. D. (1958). *Commitment To Freedom: The Story of the Christian
    Science Monitor.* Boston, Massachusetts: Houghton Mifflin
    Company.

Carcasson, M. (Spring 1998). Herbert Hoover and the Presidential Campaign
    of 1932: the Failure of Apologia. *Presidential Studies Quarterly,
    Volume 28, No. 2*, 349 - 365.

Christian Fong, N. M. (2017). *Political Legacies.* Palo Alto, California:
    Stanford University.

Christian Fong, N. M. (2017). *Political Legacies.* Palso Alto, California:
    Stanford University Graduate School of Business.

Churchill, W. (n.d.). *Courage.* Retrieved May 2020, from
    https://www.fearlessmotivation.com/2015/12/18/17-of-the-most-
    powerful-notes-on-courage/

Cohen, J. E. (2003). Greatness as Seen in the Mass Public: an Extension and
    Application of the Simonton Model. *Presidential Studies Quarterly,
    Volume 33, No. 4*, 913 - 924.

Cole, W. S. (2000, February). *Norris, George William.* Retrieved June 20,
    2020, from American National Biography:
    https://www.anb.org/view/10.1093/anb/9780198606697.001.0001/
    anb-9780198606697-e-0600476?rskey=MUO9Ix&result=2

Consistency. (n.d.). Retrieved May 2020, from www.merriam-
    webster.com/dictionary/consistency

Cordi, S. F. (n.d.). *The Colors of Sunset and Twilight.* Retrieved February
    2020, from https://www.spc.noaa.gov/publications/cordifi/sunset

Coric, S. (2017, October 24). *The Key To Success.* Retrieved May 2020, from
    http://www.medium.com/launch-school/consistency-the-key-to-
    success

Council, N. L. (1940). *Nebraska Blue Book.* Lincoln, Nebraska: State of
    Nebraska.

(1934). *County Fairgrounds Improvement McCook.* Lincoln, Nebraska:
    History Nebraska, Nebraska State Historical Society.

Courage. (n.d.). Retrieved May 2020, from https://www.merriam-
    webser.com/dictionary/courage

Crowds Mass At McCook to Hear Governor Roosevelt. (1932, September 29).
    Lincoln Star, p. 1.

Cynthia G. Emrich, H. H. (2001). Presidential Rhetoric, Charisma and Greatness. *Administrative Science Quaarterly, Volume 46, Number 3*, 527 - 557.

Democratic Leaders Are Hard Put to Find an Open Car for Roosevelt. (1932, September 28). *Omaha World-Herald*, p. 8.

Denney, J. (1961, May 14). Centennial Year for Norris. *Omaha World-Herald*, p. 102.

Dobel, J. P. (May - June 1990, May - June). Integrity in the Public Service. *Public Administration Review*, 354 - 366.

Donald, A. D. (1966). *John F. Kennedy and the New Frontier*. New York, New York: Hill and Wang.

Einstein, A. (n.d.). *Wise Old Sayings*. Retrieved May 2020, from www.wiseoldsayings.com/selfless-quotes

Eldot, P. (2000, February). *Wagner, Robert F.* Retrieved from American National Biography: https://doi.org/10.1093/anb/9780198606697.article.0600678

Eskew, C. (2014, May 13). A Question of Morality in Politics. *Washington Post*.

Expenditures, S. C. (1964). *Pageant Magazine Article*. Washington, D.C.: U.S. Government Printing Office.

FDR Whistle-Stopping in Goodland, Kansas. (n.d.). Retrieved June 2020, from http://spiritualpilgrim.net/03_The-World-since1900/05_Depression/05b_FDR-Takes-up-the-Challenge-2.htm

Feller, D. (n.d.). *Andrew Jackson: Impact and Legacy*. Retrieved June 2020, from https://www.millercenter.org/president/jackson/impact-and-legacy

Fellman, D. (1946). The Liberalism of Senator Norris. *American Political Science Review, Volume 40, Number 1*, 43.

Felzenberg, A. S. (2008). *The Leaders We Deserved (And A Few We Didn't)*. New York: Basic Books.

Fisher, G. F. (1932, September 29). Roosevelt at McCook. *Lincoln Star*, p. 13.

Flynt, W. (Winter 1972 - 1973). A Vignette in Southern Labor Politics - The 1936 Mississippi Senatorial Primary. *The Mississippi Quarterly, Volume 26, Number 1*, 89 - 99.

Folsom, B. (2009, April 24). *The Leaders We Deserved*. Retrieved June 19, 2020, from https://fee.org/articles/the-leaders-we-deserved-and-a-few-we-didnt-rethinking-the-presidential-rating-game/

Gableman, E. W. (1932, September 29). After You. *Cincinnatti Inquirer*, p. 9.

Genovese, T. E. (2013). *The Paradoxes of the American Presidency (Fourth Edition)*. Oxford, U.K.: Oxford University Press.

Bibliography

Gide, A. (2015, December 18). *Courage*. Retrieved May 2020, from
https://www/fearlessmotivation.com/2015/12/18-of-the-most-powerful-notes-on-courage/

Gilbert, R. E. (Winter 1985, Volume 15, No. 1). Personality, Stress and Achievement: Keys to Presidential Longevity. *Presidential Studies Quarterly*, 33 - 50.

Golay, M. (2013). *America 1933: The Great Depression, Lorena Hickok, Eleanor Roosevelt, and the Shaping of the New Deal.* New York, New York: Simon and Schuster.

Goldberg, R. A. (2017). *The 100: A Ranking of the Most Influential People in American History.* Boston, Massachusetts: American Publishers.

Google.com. (n.d.). Retrieved June 20, 2020, from
https://www.google.com/search?q=when+was+sunset+at+mccook+nebraska+on+september+28+1932&rlz=1C5CHFA_enUS509US509&oq=when+was+sunset+at+mccook+nebraska+on+september+28+1932&aqs=chrome..69i57.12082j0j4&sourceid=chrome&ie=UTF-8

Gormly, J. L. (July 1978). Secretary of State James F. Byrnes, an Initial British Evaluation. *The South Carolina Historical Magazine, Volume 79, Number 3*, 198 - 205.

Governor To Make Stop To See Norris. (1932, September 18). *New York Times*, p. 33.

Green, J. C. (October 1986). Presidential Leadership and the Resurgence of Trust in Government. *British Journal of Political Scoemce, Colume 16, Number 4*, 431 - 453.

Greene, S. (2001). The Role of Character Assessments in Presidential Approval. *American Politics Quarterly 29*, 196 - 210.

Grofman, S. L. (September 1988). Ideological Consistency as a Collective Phenomenom. *The American Political Science Review, Volume 82, No. 3*, 773 - 788.

Gwilt, J. (1826). *The Architecture of Marcus Vitruvius in Ten Books.* London, England: Priestley and Weale.

Hachey, T. E. (Winter 1973 - 1974). American Profiles on Capitol Hill: A Confidential Study for the British Foreign Office. *The Wisconsin Magazine of History, Volume 57, No. 2*, pp. 141 - 153.

Hagerty, J. A. (1932, September 29). Roosevelt Urges End Of Party Lines. *New York Times*, p. 10.

Halt Broadcast of McCook Program. (1932, September 29). *Omaha World-Herald*, p. 2.

Harrison Rebuffs Klan. (1927, August 27). *New York Times*, p. 14.

Harrison, Byron Patton (Pat). (n.d.). Retrieved from U. S. House of Representatives History: https://history.house.gov/People/Detail/14613

Hart, M. H. (1978). *The 100: A Ranking of the Most Influential Persons in History*. New York, New York: Kensington Publishing Corporation.

Hein, L. (2002, February 1). Remembering A True Gentleman. *McCook Gazette*, p. 1.

Henry Clay Greatest U.S. Senator. (1986, May 5). *New York Times*, p. 35.

Hickok, L. A. (1932, September 29). "It Seems Like Old Times" Greets Roosevelt As Norris Boards Train. *Nebraska State Journal*, p. 4.

Historic Ranking of Presidents of the United States. (2005, August 16). Retrieved June 19, 2020, from Wikipedia: https://en.wikipedia.org/wiki/Historical_rankings_of_presidents_of_the_United_States

Historical Rankings of Presidents of the United States. (n.d.). Retrieved 2020 June , from https:en.wikipedia.org/wiki/Historical_rankings_of_presidents_of_the_United_States

Homes, J. E. (Summer 1989). Our Best and Worst Presidents: Some Possible Reason for Perceived Performance. *Presidential Studies Quarterly, Volume 19, No. 3*, 529 - 557.

Houck, D. W. (Fall 2004). FDR's Commonwealth Club Address: Redefining Individualism, Adjudicating Greatness. *Rhetoric and Public Affairs, Volume 7, No. 3*, pp. 259 - 282.

Huthmacher, J. (July 1970). Senator Robert F. Wagner and the Rise of Urban Liberalism. *The Pacific Northwest Journal, Volume 61, Number 3*, 180 - 181.

Hyman, S. (1953, December 13). What Makes a Strong President. *New York Times*, p. 285.

Ingersoll, R. G. (n.d.). *Selections From His Oratory and Writings*. Retrieved 2020, from https://bartleby.com/400/prose/1827.html

Integrity. (n.d.). Retrieved May 2020, from https://www.merriam-webster.com/dictionary/integrity

J. Clark Archer, R. E. (2017). *Atlas of Nebraska*. Lincoln, Nebraska: University of Nebraska Press.

James F. Byrnes. (n.d.). Retrieved from Wikipedia: https://en.wikipedia.org/wiki/James_F._Byrnes

James F.Byrnes. (1972, April 10). *New York Times*, p. 34.

James Francis Byrnes. (September 1945). *American Bar Association Journal, Volume 31, Number 9*, 459 - 460.

Bibliography

Jay, J. (n.d.). *The Federalist Papers, Number 64, Gutenberg Project.* Retrieved July 2020, from https://www.gutenberg.org/files?1404/1404-h/h.htm#link2H_4_0064

Jefferson, T. (n.d.). *From Thomas Jefferson to Charles Thomson, 20 September 1787.* Retrieved from Founders Online, U.S. National Archives: https://founders.archives.gov/documents/Jefferson/01-12-02-0152#:~:text=The%20moment%20a%20person%20forms,till%20mo re%20facts%20are%20collected.

Jefferson, T. (n.d.). *Thomas Jefferson Encyclopedia.* Retrieved from monticello.org: https://www.monticello.org/site/research-and-collections/no-man-will-ever-bring-out-of-office-reputation-which carries-him-it

Jennings, R. B. (January - February 1969). Image and Integrity in the Public Service. *Public Administration Review, Volume 49, No. 1,* 74 - 77.

John Milton Cooper, J. (October 1965). William E. Borah, Political Thespian. *The Pacific Northwest Quarterly, Volume 56, Number 4,* 145 - 153.

Johnson, C. O. (January 1953). William E. Borah: the People's Choice. *The Pacific Northwest Quarterly, Volume 44, Number 1,* 15 - 22.

Jonathan Renshon, A. D. (April 2018, Volume 62, Number 2). Local Influence and Reputation formation in World Politics. *American Journal of Political Science,* 325 - 339.

Joseph P. Kennedy Roosevelt Advisor. (1932, September 24). *Boston Globe,* p. 5.

Jr., T. L. (2000, February 6). Who's a "Great" President? *The Baltimore Sun.* Baltimore: The Baltimore Sun Newspaper.

Kahn, R. L. (1937). *Integrity, the Life of George W. Norris.* New York, New York: Vanguard Press.

Kennedy, J. F. (1957, April 14). Search For The Five Greatest Senators. *New York Times.*

Krause, D. P. (2012 , January/February). Reputation and Public Administration. *Public Administration Review, Volume 72, Number 1,* 26 - 32.

Lane, L. (2011, January 9). Remembering JFK's Farewell Speech To Massachusetts . *Patriot Ledger.*

Levine, R. A. (2002, June 5). From Roosevelt to Bush: What makes a strong president? *New York Times.*

Lindgren, J. (2000). *The Federal Society and the Wall Street Journal Present: Rating The Presidents of the United States, 1789 - 2000, A Survey of*

Scholars in History, Political Science, and Law. Washington D.C.: Federalist Society.

Lissandrello, S. (1975, July 29). *Senator George W. Norris Home, National Register of Historic Places Nomination Form.* Washington, D.C.: US Department of the Interior.

Locke, W. (1945). George W. Norris, Independent. *The Antioch Review, Volume V, Number 2,* 274 - 284.

Long, B. B. (n.d.). *Red Willow County Courthouse.* Washington, D.C.: U. S. Department of the Interior.

Lowitt, R. (1969). A Case Study in Biographical Research: George W. Norris. *The Journal of Library History, Volume 4, Number 2,* 123 - 132.

Lyons, M. (1997). Presidential Character Revisited. *Political Psychology, Volume 18, Number 4,* 791 - 811.

Maddox, R. J. (n.d.). *Borah, William Edgar, American National Biography.* Retrieved July 2020, 2020, from https://doi.org/10.1093/anb/9780198606697.article.0600056

Madson, J. (1978, October). Land of Long Sunsets: Nebraska Sand Hills. *National Geographic Magazine,* pp. 493 - 517.

Maranell, G. M. (June 1970). The Evaluation of Presidents: An Extension of the Schlesinger Polls. *The Journal of American History, Volume 57, No. 1,* 104 - 113.

Marcus, R. B. (1980, March). Moral Dilemmas and Consistency. *The Journal of Philosophy,* 121 - 136.

Margaret Hurd Bride of Forrest Browne Burbank. (1934, June 9). *Lincoln Star,* p. 2.

McAvoy, G. E. (2008, June). Substance Versus Style: Distinguishing Presidential Job Performance from Favorability. *Presidential Studies Quarterly, Volume 38, Number 2,* pp. 284 - 299.

McCook All Ready to Entertain Roosevelt. (1932, September 28). *Lincoln Journal Star,* p. 10.

McCook Daily Gazette, Centennial Edition (1882 - 1982). (1982). McCook, Nebraska: McCook Daily Gazette.

McCook Ready to Greet Roosevelt. (1932, September 28). *Lincoln Journal Star,* p. 1.

McCook, Nebraska. (2015, February 12). Retrieved June 20, 2020, from https://en.wikipedia.org/wiki/McCook,_Nebraska

McKeown, A. D. (Spring 2012). The Heart of the Profession: Understanding Public Service Values. *Journal of Public Affairs Education, Volume 18, No. 2,* 375 - 396.

Bibliography

McWilliams, C. (n.d.). *McCook YMCA, Red River County, Nebraska.* Washington, D.C.: U.S. Department of the Interior.

Mengisen, A. (2008, October 31). *The Presidents Ranked and Graded with the Author of the Leaders We Deserved.* Retrieved June 19, 2020, from https://freakonomics.com/2008/10/31/the-presidents-ranked-and-graded-a-qa-with-the-author-of-the-leaders-we-deserved/

Merry, R. W. (2012, July 2). *In Pursuit of the Presidential Pantheon.* Retrieved June 19, 2020, from Wall Street Journal: https://www.wsj.com/articles/SB10001424052702303561504577494952787447554

Milkis, S. (n.d.). *Theodore Roosevelt: Impact and Legacy.* Retrieved June 2020, from https://www.millercenter.org/president/theodoreroosevelt/impact-and-legacy

Miller, K. (n.d.). *The West: The Lion of Idaho... William E. Borah, More Than A Little American.* Retrieved July 2020, from http://hnn.us/articles/636.html

Morgan, T. S. (Summer 1994). James F. Byrnes and the Politics of Segregation. *The Historian*, pp. 645 - 654.

Morgan, T. S. (Summer 1994). James F. Byrnes and the Politics of Segregation. *The Historian, Volume 56, Number 4*, 645 - 654.

Morris, G. O. (1982). *McCook's First Hundred Years: A Centennial Collection of Historical Highlights From McCook, Nebraska.* McCook, Nebraska: High Plains Historical Society.

Nebraska, F. W. (1939). *Nebraska: A Guide to the Cornhusker State - Tour 8 B (McCook).* New York: Viking Press.

Nelson, M. (2013). *The Presidency and the Executive Branch, Fifth Edition, Volume 1.* Thousand Oaks, California: Sage Publications.

Newman, B. (2003). Integrity and Presidential Approval. *Public Opinion Quarterly 67*, 335 - 367.

Newman, B. (June 2004). "The Polls":Presidential Traits and Job Approval: Some Aggregate-Level Evidence. *Presidential Studies Quarterly*, 437 - 448.

Newmark, J. L. (Fall 2002, Volume 2, Number 3). A Dynamic Model of U.S. Senator Approval, 1981 - 2000. *State Politics and Policy quarterly*, pp. 298 - 316.

Norris Called Ideal Liberal by Roosevelt. (1932, September 29). *Baltimore Sun*, p. 1.

Norris Glad to be Home. (1932, September 23). *Lincoln Journal Star*, p. 7.

The Sunset At McCook

Norris Introduces Roosevelt At McCook. (1932, September 29). *Omaha World-Herald*, p. 1.

Norris, G. (Second Session). The Spider Web of Wall Street. *The Congressional Record, 72nd Congress, 2nd Session, Volume 76, Part T*, 4769 - 4780.

Norris, G. W. (1945). *Fighting Liberal: The Autobiography of George W. Norris.* Lincoln, Nebraska: University of Nebraska Press.

Onuf, P. (n.d.). *Thomas Jefferson : Impact and Legacy.* Retrieved June 2020, from https://www.millercenter.org/president/jefferson/impact-and-legacy

Oppenheimer, L. C. (1997). *Congress Reconsidered.* Washington, D. C.: Congressional Quarterly Inc.

Osburn, K. M. (Winter 2008). Mississippi Choctaws and Racial Politics. *University of North Carolina Press*, 32 - 54.

Partin, J. W. (November 1979). Roosevelt, Byrnes, and the 1944 Vice-Presidential Nomination. *The Historian, Volume 42, Number 1*, 85 - 100.

Pat Harrison. (n.d.). Retrieved from Wikipedia: https://en.wikipedia.org/wiki/Pat_Harrison

Pat Harrison. (n.d.). Retrieved from Find A Grave: https://www.findagrave.com/memorial/8004327/pat-harrison

Pat Harrison (Politician). (n.d.). Retrieved from Mississippi Encyclopedia: http://mississippiencyclopedia.org/

Pat of the Senate. (1922, July 9). *New York Times*, p. S 83.

Peirce, N. R. (1972). *The Great Plains States of America: People, Politics and Power in the Nine Great Plains States.* New York, New York: W. W. Norton.

Photo of FDR and Campaign Entourage. (n.d.). Retrieved May 2020, from https://fdrlibrary.files.wordpress.com/2013/11/roosevelt-kennedy_2.jpg

Plischke, E. (1985). Rating Presidents and Diplomats In Chief. *Presidential Studies Quarterly*, 725 - 742.

Political Ethics. (n.d.). Retrieved June 2020, from https://www.en.wikipedia.org/wiki/Political_ethics

R.F.D. to F.D.R. (1937, January 11). *Time Magazine*, pp. 16 - 19.

Ragsdale, W. B. (1932, September 29). Nebraska Solon Bolts To Back Democrats. *Owensboro Messenger*, p. 2.

Ragsdale, W. B. (1932, September 29). Norris Praises Governor Roosevelt As Needed Man. *Lincoln Journal Star*, p. 2.

Bibliography

Raymond Charles Moley. (n.d.). Retrieved May 2020, from
 https://en.wikipedia.org/wiki/Raymond_Moley

Red Willow County Fair Sunset. (2017, July). Retrieved June 2020, from
 Facebook.com

Riccio, B. D. (August 1990). The U.S. Presidency and the "Ratings Game".
 The Historian, 566 583.

Riley, S. G. (1995). *Biographical Dictionary of American Newspaper
 Columnists.* Westport, Connecticut: Greenwood Press.

Robert F. Wagner. (n.d.). Retrieved from Wikipedia:
 https://en.wikipedia.org/wiki/Robert_F._Wagner

Robert F. Wagner Dies At The Age of 75. (1953, May 5). *New York Times*,
 p. 1.

Romero, V. (2014). Of Love and Hate: Understanding the Determinants of
 Presidential Legacies. *Political Science Quarterly, Volume 67,
 Number 1*, 123 - 135.

Ronald C. Naugle, J. J. (2014). *History of Nebraska, Fourth Edition.* Lincoln,
 Nebraska: University of Nebraska Press.

Roosevelt Headquarters Campaign Special. (1932, September 16).
 Birmingham News, p. 2.

Roosevelt, F. D. (n.d.). *Bellefontaine, Ohio - Whistlestop Remarks (Speech
 File 494).* Retrieved May 2020, from
 http://www.fdrlibrary.marist.edu/_resources/images/msf/msf00596

Roosevelt, F. D. (n.d.). *Franklin D. Roosevelt, "The Great Communicator"
 The Master Speech Files, Series 1, File No. 593, 1932, November 7,
 Poughkeepsie, NY - Informal Speech.* Retrieved June 20, 2020, from
 Speeches of Franklin Delano Roosevelt:
 http://www.fdrlibrary.marist.edu/archives/collections/franklin/index
 .php?p=collections/findingaid&id=582

Roosevelt, F. D. (n.d.). *Franklin Delano Roosevelt Master Speech File (1898 -
 1945).* Retrieved 2020 May, from
 http://fdrlibrary.marist.edu/archives/collections/franklin/index.php?
 p=collections/findaid&id=582

Roosevelt, F. D. (n.d.). *Poughkeepsie, New York Informal Speech.* Retrieved
 June 2020, from Franklin Delano Roosevelt Library.

Roosevelt, F. D. (n.d.). *Renomination Speech for the Presidency.* Retrieved
 from The American Presidency Project:
 https://presidency.ucsb.edu/documents/acceptance-speech-for-the-
 renomination-for-the-presidency-philadelphia-pa

Roosevelt, T. (n.d.). *Courage.* Retrieved May 2020, from
https://www.fearlessmotivation.com/2015/12/18/17-of-the-most-
powerful-notes-on-courage/

Roosevelt's Speech At McCook. (1932, September 29). *New York Times*, p.
10.

Roosevelt's Train Sets New Record For Speed. (1932, September 29).
Knoxville News-Sentinel, p. 14.

Rosenman, S. L. (1952). *Working with Roosevelt.* London: Rubert Hart-
Davis.

Rossiter, C. (1960). *The American Presidency.* New York, New York: The
New American Library of World Literature, Inc.

Ryan, H. (1995). *U. S. Presidents As Orators.* Westport, Connecticut:
Greenwood Press.

Ryan, H. R. (1988). *Franklin D. Roosevelt's Rhetorical Presidency.* New
York: Greenwood Press.

Sehnert, W. E. (2000). *Ray Search Remembers McCook.* Kearny, Nebraska:
Morris Publishing.

Senator George W. Norris. (1937, January 11). *Time*, p. 16.

Senator Harrison Honored in Capitol. (1941, June 24). *New York Times*, p.
20.

Senator Norris To Welcome Demo Chief To State. (1932, September 29).
Lincoln Star, p. 1.

Shakespeare, W. (n.d.). *Twelfth Night, Act 2, Scene 5.* Retrieved May 2020,
from Brainy Quotes:
http://www.brainyquote.com/quotes/william_shakespeare_101484

Shaw, J. T. (n.d.). *When John F. Kennedy Judged the Senate's Greats.*
Retrieved June 2020, from https://www.historynewsnetwork.org

Siena Research Institute, S. C. (2019). *America's Presidents: Greatest and
Worst.* Loudonville, New York: Siena College.

Simonton, D. K. (August 2006). Presidential IQ, Openness, Intellectual
Brilliance, and Leadership: Estimates and Correlaations for 42 U.S.
Chief Executives. *Political Psychology, Volume 27, No. 4*, 511 - 526.

Simonton, D. K. (June 1986). Presidential Greatness: The Historic Consensus
and Its Psychological Significance. *Political Psychology, Volume 7,
No. 2*, 259 - 283.

Simonton, D. K. (Spring 1991). Greatness: An Alternative to the Kenney and
Rice Contextual Index. *Presidential Studies Quarterly, Volume 21,
No. 2*, 301 - 305.

Skiles, S. (2007). *McCook Memories.* McCook, Nebraska: McCook Daily
Gazette.

Bibliography

Sorensen, T. (2008). *Counselor: A Life at the Edge of History*. New York, New York: Harper .

Strout, R. L. (1979). *TRB: Views and Perspectives On The Presidency*. New York, New York: Macmillan Publishing Company.

Strout, R. L. (1983, October 23). *The Enduring Legacy of Franklin Roosevelt.* Retrieved February 2020, from http://www.washingtonpost.com/archive/entertainment/books/1983/10/23/the-enduring-legacy-of-franklin-d-roosevelt/732914d-a983-4cd2-aff3-2519bc0939be/

Strunk, A. D. (1982). *Centennial Edition (1882 - 1932)*. McCook, Nebraska: McCook Daily Gazette.

Swain, M. H. (2000, February). *Harrison, Pat.* Retrieved from American National Biography: https://doi.org/10.1093/anb/9780198606697.article.0600257

Swain, M. H. (n.d.). *Senator Pat Harrison: Nw Deal Wheelhorse (1933 - 1941) Suspicious of His Load*. Retrieved from History Now: http://www.mshistorynow.mdah.ms.gov/?articles/374/senator-pat-harrison-new-deal-wheelhorse-suspicious-of-his-load-1933-1941

Swain, M. H. (Winter 1977 - 1978). The Harrison Education Bills, 1936 - 1941. *The Mississippi Quarterly*, 119 - 131.

The Leaders We Deserved. (2020, June 19). Retrieved June 19, 2020, from Wikipedia: https://en.wikipedia.org/wiki/The_Leaders_We_Deserved

The Progressive Era. (n.d.). Retrieved June 2020, from https://xourses.lumenlearning.org

Thies, G. M. (Summer 2016). Reputation Overrides Record: How Warren G. Harding mistakenly became the "worst" President of the United States. *The Independent Reivew, Volume 21, No. 1*, 29 - 45.

Thomas P. Wolf, W. D. (2001). *Franklin D. Roosevelt and Congress: The New Deal and Its Aftermath*. New York: M. E. Sharpe.

Thomas, J. R. (1990, February). The Modern United States Senate: What is Accorded Respect. *The Journal of Politics, Volume 52, Number 1*, pp. 126 - 145.

Thousands Gather at McCook to Jollify over Work Done. (1932, September 29). *Lincoln Star*, p. 4.

Tobin, R. L. (1961). *Decisions of Destiny*. New York, New York: Avon Book Division, Hearst Publishing.

TRB. (1982, September 27). Adventure In Socialism. *Baltimore Sun*, p. 11.

Unamuno, M. d. (1921). *Tragic Sense of Life*. Mineola, New York: Dover Publications.

Underhill, R. (2014). *Against The Grain: Six Men Who Shaped America*. New York, New York: Algora Publishing.

Unselfishness. (n.d.). Retrieved May 2020, from www.vocabulary.com/dictionary/unselfishness

Vivekananda, S. (n.d.). *Wise Old Sayings*. Retrieved May 2020, from www.wiseoldssayings.com/selfless-quotes

Walsh, D. J. (1932, September 28). Gotham All Set To Start Series. *Lincoln Star*, p. 11.

Washington Correspondents Name Ablest Congressmen in Life Poll. (1939, March 20). *Life Volume 6 Number 12*, pp. 13 - 17.

Washington Correspondents Name Ablest Congressmen in Life Poll. (1939, March 28). *Life*, pp. 13 - 18.

Washington, G. (n.d.). *Conversation with Alexander Hamitlon, August 28, 1788*. Retrieved May 2020, from www.mountvernon.org/library/digitalhistory/quotes/

Webb, W. P. (1931). *The Great Plains*. Lincoln, Nebraska: University of Nebraska Press.

West, L. L. (1968, July). The Defeat of George W. Norris in the 1942 Nebraska. *Master of Arts Thesis, Oklahoma State University*.

What Makes A Great Senator. (1945, July 17). *Dayton Daily News*, p. 12.

White, R. (n.d.). *Wise Old Sayings*. Retrieved May 2020, from http://wiseoldsayings.com/selfless-quotes

Wickenden, D. (1994). *The New Republic Reader: Eighty Years of Opinion and Debate*. New York, New York: Harper Collins.

Wildavsky, R. E. (Winter 1991). "Greatness" Revisited: Evaluating the Performance of Early American Presidents in Terms of Cultural Dilemmas. *Presidential Studies Quarterly, Volume 21, No. 1*, 15 - 34.

Wiley. (1955). *Provisions of Federal Statutes, Executive Orders, and Congressional Resolution Relating to the Internal Security of the United States*. Washington D.C.: United States Government Printing Office.

William Borah. (n.d.). Retrieved July 2020, from https://en.wikipedia.org/wiki/William_Borah

Wilson Legacy, the American Experience. (n.d.). Retrieved June 2020, from https://www.pbs.org/wgbh/americanexperience/features/wilson-legacy/

Winfred B. Moore, J. (April 1983). James F. Byrnes: The Road to Politics, 1882 - 1910. *The South Carolina Historical Magazine, Volume 84, Number 2*, 72 - 88.

Bibliography

Wise Integrity Quotes. (n.d.). Retrieved May 2020, from
    https://www.wiseoldsayings.com/integrity-quotes

Wiseman, C. V. (2018). *Legislative Effectiveness in the United States Senate.*
    Vanderbilt University and the University of Virginia.

World-Herald, O. (1932, September 29). Halt Broadcast of McCook Program.
    Omaha World-Herald, p. 2.

Yu, L. (2005, November). The Great Communicator: How FDR's Radio
    Speeches Shaped American History. *The History Teacher, Volume
    39, No. 1,* pp. 89 - 106.

Zimmerman, J. F. (September 1982). Ethics in the Public Service. *State and
    Local Government Review, Volume 14, Number 3,* 98 - 106.

Zucker, N. L. (1966). *George W. Norris: Gentle Giant of American
    Democracy.* Urbana, Illinois: University of illinois Press.

Index

Index

Index

Index